CW01497645

There Is No Meant to Be

There Is No Meant to Be

~~A memoir~~

~~A novel~~

A family story

JARRED McGINNIS

HARVILL

1 3 5 7 9 10 8 6 4 2

Harvill, an imprint of Vintage, is part of the
Penguin Random House group of companies

Vintage, Penguin Random House UK, One Embassy Gardens,
8 Viaduct Gardens, London SW11 7BW

penguin.co.uk/vintage
global.penguinrandomhouse.com

Penguin
Random House
UK

First published by Harvill in 2026

Copyright © Jarred McGinnis 2026

The moral right of the author has been asserted

Typeset in 11.8/16.2pt Calluna by Six Red Marbles UK, Thetford, Norfolk
Printed and bound in Great Britain by Clays Ltd, Elcograf S.p.A.

The authorised representative in the EEA is Penguin Random House Ireland,
Morrison Chambers, 32 Nassau Street, Dublin D02 YH68

A CIP catalogue record for this book is available from the British Library

ISBN 9781787303850

Penguin Random House is committed to a sustainable future
for our business, our readers and our planet. This book is made
from Forest Stewardship Council® certified paper.

In memory of Jane, Vikki and Kim.
The other mothers I have known.

The First American

In the middle of the nineteenth century, the three McGinnis brothers fled to America from County Down, Ireland, and a conviction for larceny of livestock. The brothers worked to point the railroads' crooked iron fingers towards the endless expanse beyond the Appalachians. When they came into town from the work camps, they got drunk. They caused problems. The locals, tired of these troublesome immigrants, rode up to the camp before sunrise and picked their way through the men and tents until they found where the McGinnis brothers slept. They marched them at gunpoint to the well of an abandoned homestead. They shot the oldest first. The interval of time between his body disappearing into the hole and the dry thud stretched to an impossible length. With the depth measured, the bodies of the younger brothers seemed to fall quicker. Meanwhile, in the belly of a village daughter, there roiled a green-eyed, black-haired son, Bishop McGinnis.

Nearly two hundred years later, Bishop's great-great-great-grandson travels from London to rural North Carolina with his wife to introduce their newly born twin daughters to the grandpa and the rest of the family. He has received no summons, but he understands what is expected from him. The father had done the same when the grandson was born forty years ago.

Surrounded by the brutal fields of cotton and tobacco, all the houses around here have McGinnises in them. The grandson half-jokingly calls this corner of Southern coastal plains 'the McGinnis Compound'. The father comes up from Florida for the visit. Having the four living generations of McGinnises together feels significant.

Recently, the father's emails talk of love, but it is God's love quarantined between quote marks and chapter and verse ascriptions. The grandson does not remember ever hearing I love you from the grandpa.

As soon as they enter the house, the grandma hugs everyone then asks if the grandson is hungry. Without waiting for his reply, she disappears into the kitchen. Her food is Southern but flecked with flavours and ingredients carried with her from Vietnam. When the grandson's wife asks for her bánh bao recipe, the grandma says that she got it from *Good Housekeeping*.

The grandpa and the father look more like brothers, both muscular, compressed springs. The grandson instinctively feels tension when he is within arm's reach of the father, not because anything is going to happen now, but from the muscle memory of when it did. The grandpa's arms and legs are still lean, but his belly belies his love of homemade pineapple wine and the grandma's pulled brisket.

When McGinnises gather, they play pinochle, an idiosyncratic game of melding and trick-taking. It was

4

popular in the nineteenth century with the newly arrived Jews and Irish. Played with two incomplete decks of cards from nines to aces, it requires lots of card memorisation. The grandson remembers playing with the father and the grandpa when he was ten. No allowances were made for his age. After misplaying a hand, he was scolded: if you're going to play a man's game, you better play it like a man.

Now, the grandson is a man, with two children of his own. He sits at the kitchen table handmade by the grandpa. He bridge-shuffles the cards and deals to the father, the grandpa and a male cousin while the aunts, wives and the grandma take turns holding the babies. The grandpa shows no interest in the newborns. But there is a moment, almost missed, when one of the twins in the grandma's arms reaches out a pudgy hand at the end of her rubber band wrist. She touches the grey high and tight haircut of the retired marine drill sergeant. The grandpa smiles and leans in for her to get a better feel. Out beyond the porch, a flock of Chinese geese honk and squawk as they waddle between persimmon trees to swim in the lake shaped by the grandpa's resolve and backhoe.

To win at pinochle you must communicate with your partner, signalling through bids and play to coordinate each other's unseen hands. As the cards are tossed and tricks gathered, the grandpa talks, partly to distract the others from him deliberately misplaying hands and taking tricks unearned. He brags about how, during a recent surgery, he threatened the surgeons with physical harm if they dared to give him morphine. The grandson laughs at the foolishness but also admires it. To endure, he has been taught, is a virtue. Twenty years ago, after a near fatal accident, he lay in the intensive care unit between a man shot in the face during an argument in a Texas roadhouse and a man hit by a train entering the United States from Mexico. The grandson would leave the unit as a paraplegic, permanently dependent on a wheelchair, but he would leave.

The grandpa declares, 'When I get to the end of infinity, I'm going to build a wall to keep the rest of you all out.' With his white beard and eye patch, this feels like a prognostication from All-Father himself.

Most of all he tells family stories. Especially about his mom. She got married when she was sixteen, fleeing from her stepmother's house where she was more servant than daughter. The grandson remembers her as a small woman, red-haired, always surrounded by an aura of kindness and mewing, scrawny cats.

She knew the small magic, the grandpa says. Neither the grandson nor anyone asks what that means.

He talks about their house, which, during his childhood, had been the family's diner and motel, the McGinnis Sho-me Courts, until Eisenhower's interstate highways diverted customers away. Their living room still had a line of circles with four bolt holes, like a row of buttons on a work shirt, from where the counter stools had been removed. The grandpa says that ghosts used to visit his mom during the diner's long empty late nights. Shifts of twenty-four hours or more were not uncommon. The dead would bring her their stories. The family discusses whether these were real or hallucinations while the grandson thinks about the dreams that he has had since he was a teenager, the dreams when the dead show him their homes.

The grandpa moves on to another story. Late one night, his mom was working alone. A man came in and ordered black coffee and grits. She had a bad feeling about him and the questions he was asking. When a regular, a game warden, saddled up to the counter, she made it clear not to leave her alone with the stranger. The next time she saw the stranger, it was his photo in the newspaper shortly after his arrest, accused of being the Route 66 Killer.

The grandson asks about the story of the three McGinnis brothers. The grandpa says that he doesn't know that one. The grandson tells it as he remembers hearing it told to him.

The Caulbearer

Fourth of July 1976, the bicentenary of the Declaration of Independence. A big day for a nation already more interested in looking back rather than forward. It was also momentous for the small town of Clovis, New Mexico, where my dad was stationed at Cannon Air Force Base. That year there were not only whispers that a Kmart store was going to be built just off US Highway 285. It was foretold that I was to be born on the bicentenary. It was inevitable: the seventh-generation firstborn son of a firstborn son of the McGinnises would arrive on that most important day for the Republic. To sweeten the deal, the local newspaper offered one hundred dollars for any military child born on the fourth. My dad took my mom off-roading on his motorcycle hoping the rough ride over canyon rocks would help improve the odds of predestination.

Alas, I didn't arrive until the eighteenth, which is the date that George Washington, the father of our nation, caught syphilis from 'a devilish passion' with a girl from Beardstown. An occasion for which no one was offering a cash prize.

The day before, my mother went to an appointment to

induce her malingering progeny. Afterwards she felt some pain, a spot of blood, but attributed it to the indelicacy of the internal examination.

She said hands that size had no place near, never mind inside, the tender parts of a young woman. She didn't know her contractions had started.

I was young. I had never been pregnant before. I didn't know, she explained.

My mother's labour began in earnest after she and my dad had gone to bed. When she woke him, he rolled over and assured her it could wait until morning. She tried to breathe through the waves of pain as they gathered force and insistence. After she armed herself with a call to the labour ward and the nurse's insistence, she dared to tell my dad that they needed to get to the hospital immediately. He grumbled awake and went to the bathroom. Mom lay in the dark, holding her belly, waiting until he returned dressed and holding the car keys.

Their emerald-green Subaru GL followed the dark and empty highway towards the base hospital. My mother rolled her window down to let in the cool desert air. A mile-long cattle train shadowed their route as it brought thousands of head to the industrial abattoirs, which, along with the Air Force, were the town's major employers. The harsh steel rattle of train against track put sound to her pain and the freshness of the night was spoiled by the stink of tons of braying meat going to slaughter. She could no longer sit. She arched away from her seat, almost standing, her belly too large for a seat belt.

Dad stopped at a gas station where an Air Force buddy's wife, soon to be my godmother, was working the night shift. Mom watched her friend unlock the front door and let him in, already willing her husband to hurry. He helped himself to one of the hot link sausages glistening on the heat-drenched rollers.

What if the baby comes and Robin's home alone? What're you doing out? she asked.

He chewed for a bit, stuffed the bite of white bread and sausage into his cheek and answered, The baby's already coming. Robin's in the car.

Even after they got to the hospital, there was a further wait for the doctor to return from a party. He told Mom it would still be a few hours so don't push until then.

I have to push, she said to the nurse after the doctor left.

You can't, said the nurse.

I have to.

You can't.

Mom pushed and the crown of my head emerged, ending the discussion. Dad's eyes bulged and he fled. The nurse caught the doctor in the parking lot and brought him back. When they put a heart monitor on my fontanelle, a scratchy static heartbeat came from the speakers.

Mom panicked, What's wrong?

Nurse, can you turn off the monitor? the doctor said.

Do it yourself, the nurse shot back.

I arrived with a thin tissue of amniotic sac still enveloping my head. This was the cause of my distress: I couldn't breathe. My mom screamed at the sight of my face in its bloody veil. The doctor flicked the mirror away so she couldn't see her deformed child. With a few more pushes and the come-hither of forceps, I was born. The doctor cleared away the caul and cleaned me up to present me to my mother. She remembers the frightening size of me. Screaming, face scrunched, bright red. Maybe it was the drugs, she told me, but you were huge, a huge head, a fleshly lollipop with ears, and a tuft of black hair on top. A nightmare.

That's not my baby. I had a tiny baby, she pleaded to the doctor.

This is your baby, ma'am.

After a few more whispers of disbelief, she settled into being my mom. It was the role she had written about most in her teenage diaries. The thing she wanted more than anything was a baby.

In Europe, a caulbearer is immune to drowning and can protect the harvest from evil spirits. In the tradition of the American South, a caul birth is a mixed blessing: it is said that the baby will be able to see and hear boggarts and haints. Ghosts. They will be prescient about death and can sense its immediacy in others.

The story my mom tells is that I glowed blue. Both Mom and Dad say that they didn't notice in the fluorescent light of the hospital but, when they brought me home and set me in the bassinet, I glowed. Dad says it was a yellow phosphorescence and the dumb military doctor thought I had jaundice. That first night, as they stood over my bassinet, my mom spoke of her fear that the Air Force had irradiated her baby.

My dad held her. No, this felt benevolent, he said. Each

night the glow, whether it was blue or yellow, dimmed, and by the third day, it was no longer visible.

I mentioned my mom's story about me glowing as a baby to Sarah, my wife.

She said, It's like you and all your superstitions.

What superstitions?

You think it's bad luck to hear about someone's pregnancy before week thirteen.

Statistically, most miscarriages happen in the first trimester.

You always tell people if they appear in your dreams, she continued, in case it might be 'useful'.

Why did you do scare quotes? I told you about my dreams. I get déjà vu dreams. You can't mess around with dreams.

Mhmm, she said, a little too smugly.

My mom too believes in foresight. She told me that she knew something bad had happened when I had my car accident. She was at her desk at work and felt the push and pull of an unexpected wave wash over her. As it drew back, a sharp pain remained in her chest. At that same moment, I was dying beneath a truck.

When I was growing up, she had an uncanny ability to know which of my friends were likely to lead me towards trouble.

No matter how hard he tries to be something else, I can tell he's a bad person, she said about a friend who generally charmed parents. He's got those smudges for eyes, that's how you know.

When she said that I thought of all the times he drank and of the nights he tipped into ugliness so that, when he disappeared, we were all grateful, even if there was a possibility he had climbed over the rails of a nearby bridge.

When our twins were born, my mom gave me a fist-sized chunk of petrified bark that Dad had found in New Mexico. Its fragility and iridescence make it easy to believe in its magic. The stone sits on our bookshelf in a glass box where it sparkles in the afternoon sun and keeps misfortune away from our daughters. Dad taught the younger me how to look for these power objects, a rock or a pine cone, anything natural, that calls to you. There is a specific feeling, hard to explain, you feel when they are near. I've taught the same lesson to the girls and, when we come home from a walk, they empty their pockets into the potted plants on our terrace, to appease the fairies.

I've read explanations for déjà vu, so I understand how the brain's implicit associations and shallow processing of an experience allows a 'seen again' experience to feel like foreknowledge. That doesn't mean I can shake those moments of dread when something happens that I've dreamt. When my mom talked about the wave of foreboding that she felt when my accident happened, I knew what she was talking about. For the dreams of the dead and their homes, I have no explanation.

The dead show me their homes but, unlike my great-grandma, they have never told me any stories. It is important to them that they show me their homes, I understand this much, and so, I follow. Their homes are bright, clear, and crisp as if seen in waking, but the colours are a hue or two off and the angles never quite right. I have wondered if these homes were the fading understandings of a place that they knew alive, but that can't be true. There is always a sense of happiness or, if not happiness, calm. I remember one of my dreams from when I was a teenager. I was shown a kitchen with linoleum flooring patterned with flowers. I recognised the purple grains of lavender stalks. A woman stood expressionless in the middle, the points of house slippers peeking from beneath the folds of a cotton dress. Beyond the window at the sink, there was a jag of black branches studded with spring buds.

Often my focus narrows to an object as if my attention is directed. In this woman's kitchen there was a seventies-era wall clock, its hands pointed towards serifed numbers reading 8:15. When in the dreams, if I try to understand what I'm being shown, it ends. I see a wooden end-table with candlesticks, a book with a title I can't make out in the dream sight. What's important about the title? Why can't I make it out? Then I'm awake, trying to recall what the dead have shown me.

A month or so before I received the email from Grandma, the dead showed me Grandpa's house, the one that he built in North Carolina. The ghost is a man, but not my grandfather. He wears an American army uniform; Grandpa was a marine. I recognise the man from a family photo. He is my ancestor, Bishop McGinnis.

In the dream, his drab greens were vivid. The living room in which we stood – and I'm never in a wheelchair in these dreams – was emptied of all the house's normal furnishing except for a single burgundy rug. We were looking at each other and I recognised my eyebrows above his eyes. They are solid, prominent brows, genetic inevitabilities. He turned his head, and I followed his gaze. The fireplace was empty and the mantel clear. I felt the comfort of this place.

Later I asked my uncle to send me a digital copy of the photo so that I could confirm whom I thought I had seen. My ancestor, a young lieutenant, stands in the background of a large group photo. Someone has written that he is the 'twelfth from the left behind young woman'. The photo is historically important because it was the largest gathering of Union generals: I recognise Sheridan's foppish moustache; Grant grimly front and centre, square hands upon the wooden picket fence; Sherman to the right in profile with a cigar pinched between his fingers. The wooden frontier house is flanked by two flags that have fluttered to a blur in the slow blink of the camera's eye. Only a striped pale candle fire and an attenuated field of stars is visible. Before the crowd is the body of a large hound whose turning head has also dissolved into smoke.

Bishop was to be the name of the first son that I didn't have, taken from this ancestor more for my love of unusual names than for his illustrious military record.

Grandpa was dead, or maybe he wasn't. I received an email from Grandma saying he was. That felt authoritative. The crying started when I tried to respond. Staring at my keyboard, searching for any words worth typing, pulled a latch and emptied me. My daughter, Zed, was asleep on the couch, splayed out like a drunk. Her twin, Maude, stopped her playing to investigate. At two years old she had the swagger of a bantamweight approaching the ring: arms straight, crab-apple fists, shoulders swinging, hips forward. She put her hands on my wheelchair and looked up into my face to comprehend her father. I played that I was laughing, as if I could protect her from ever knowing sadness. How physically similar laughing and crying are. When she giggled, I no longer had to pretend. She squealed with pleasure at her silly Papa and ran off, unsteady, lurching, adorable, and I chased after her. I felt the hollowness still but also the joy that toddlers radiate. When we recall a moment, there is the need to fix it to a single emotion, but when is that ever true?

I called Dad. I needed to talk to family.

I asked if he was okay.

He responded by talking about his day's itinerary. He was about to leave for tai chi.

In the gap made by my stunned silence, he said he was about to call me. He had just spoken to his sister, and they were making Grandpa as comfortable as possible, but they were not going to operate on the brain haemorrhage. Surgery would leave him a vegetable. Neither Grandpa nor anyone else wanted that. I was confused. I told him about the email from Grandma saying that he was dead.

Oh yeah? he said.

I doubted myself now. Could I have misunderstood Grandma's email? We concluded that most likely, yes, he had passed, and I joked that if anyone was harder than death, it was Grandpa.

Is there going to be a service? I asked. The flights will be expensive, but I want to be there.

Dad said something about Grandpa not wanting a service or Grandpa saying Dad wouldn't be invited anyway. I didn't quite understand but his response sounded like shutters slamming. I didn't push.

He said his wife was hurrying him to go.

Okay, I said.

Three days later, I hadn't heard from anyone. I kept checking family members' social media. Nothing. Grandpa's page was full of anti-Trump links. I understood the outrage, but I wished there was more of him there. I wanted his infrared video clips of wildlife visiting his feeders or one of his tortured puns. Scrolling down further, on the day before he died, I saw Grandpa had posted a picture that I had taken of my two daughters beneath the Eiffel Tower. A woman had commented, 'And (they) will not remember it.' The pointless shittiness of this made me laugh. Grandpa immediately defended his boast by bragging that his great-granddaughters had been to more countries than he had been to US states.

A week later, I got more of the story of what happened. Despite losing an arm last year to sarcoma and being back on chemo, Grandpa still built furniture. He had rigged the workshop to accommodate his disability. Through-out the last year, he had been emailing me pictures of motorcycles that could be driven one-handed. The day he died, he had fallen down the stairs in his workshop and spiked his head onto a sharp-cornered metal workbench. After he regained consciousness, he dragged himself into the house, and he phoned his brother's wife who lived next door. She waited for the ambulance with him. When the paramedics asked what happened, he pointed to her and said, She hit me with a skillet!

I most often thought about the blood trail from his workshop into the house. I imagined the evidence that would be left by an 83-year-old man with one arm, bleeding out from a head wound. The trail his knees made through the grass. Someone, Grandma or an aunt, would have had to wash the blood from the steps, from the door, from the phone.

In an email, Grandma described how he kept the doctors and nurses laughing until he was unrespon-sive. *They thought he was remarkable. And they were right. He was very proud of you all. His last email to me was about Sarah's new job. He loved you, Jarred. He loved his great-granddaughters. He would have said to us, do not cry, I will see you on the other side of infinity.*

Grandpa had been cremated with no ceremony, according to his wishes. Grandma offered me one of the coffee tables that he had made. Dad agreed to retrieve and store it – probably indefinitely because we no longer live in America and have no intention of returning. My aunt sent me a notebook that Grandpa had written to me over the first years of my life. Not quite a letter but a diary addressed to his first grandson, the first son of his first son. It takes up an entire stenographer's notebook. Its cover has no mark from Grandpa, only the promise of 'SPE-CIALLY SELECTED PAPER' from the manufacturer. The spiral binding is a little smooshed from forty-plus years of storage. The first entry, several pages long, is in a deliberate and neat cursive. Halfway through the entries become urgent and all caps before relaxing into a harder-to-read print near the end. The pen changes through the entries. He had taped into the notebook letters from my dad to him. Dad's handwriting is always a sharp cursive resembling a seismograph's output.

Several times Grandpa wrote about obeying your parents, and I think about his dominance of my father and what that has wrought. The Bible verses he quoted (Hebrews 12) were about enduring beatings and being resilient against suffering. He liked proverbs and unwieldy metaphors. That did not change throughout his writing over the forty years I knew him. Grandpa's voice occasionally emerged from the aphorisms pilfered from scripture and cod philosophy, and some of his advice tugged at me because of my need for its resonance. *Try to look back once in a while and see where you went right. That will give you a line on where you should go next.* Though he wrote these words during my first year of life, there are times it felt that he knew this would be read after his death and with a specific purpose. *I suppose as you read this you have a much different impression of what is being said than I do.*

He wrote to my newborn self that my actions must honour the name McGinnis. I'm aware of the old-fashioned silliness of this. There is no castle or title associated with the descendants of Irish peasants from the rural American South. When my grandfather went to the village that we McGinnises supposedly left in the nineteenth century, he asked a local if he knew the family and was told, Horse thieves, the lot of them. Whether true, or a standby response for the predictable questions of American tourists, that story has been added to the family lore.

He writes that if I never bring shame to the name his father has handed down to me through him and my father, I will wear that name as a suit of armour. I don't remember him or my dad teaching me this lesson explicitly, but I have found myself saying to my daughters, But, of course, you're a McGinnis, as a form of praise at some child-sized success.

My favourite entries are references to family goings-on over the years. He fondly recalls a visit from my dad. I was a sickly child, and he writes of his grandfatherly concerns. *Now they are saying it is asthma, but I have my doubts.* It was asthma. Grandpa always had lots of jobs:

24

he writes that he works at a high school, manages his and other people's properties, and teaches self-hypnosis twice a week. The entry about him being a professional gambler is true, because I have a memory of him taking me to the horse track and watching a tractor pull a curtain in front of a fallen animal before a man in a baseball cap shot it.

On the day I was born, he wrote that he was sitting on the floor at his front door to catch a cool breeze and relief from the Florida summer. I see my 39-year-old Grandpa shirtless with the notepad propped against his knee as he writes to his new grandson. Near the end, some ninety pages later, he veers close to poetry. *As I write a man roams the moon.*

I understand that immediate need to write to a newborn. I have several unfinished letters to my daughters. I have never finished them because, unlike my grandpa, I want to find out who they are and not dictate who I want them to be. Why did Grandpa never send me his letter? Was it waning enthusiasm as a newborn becomes a toddler becomes a child becomes an adult? Maybe he was planning on sending it after I had children of my own and then forgot because it took forty years to give him great-grandchildren. I don't know.

You will be expected to visit them [his father and mother, my great-grandparents] *this first Thanksgiving of yours in 1976,* he wrote to newborn me, *They will be waiting with open arms.* My young parents obediently made the eight-hundred-mile journey, because later in the letter in a section dated December 1976, Grandpa reported, *I found you to be a very pleasant and happy baby. One day they were trying to get you to take a nap and nothing worked. I went to your crib and made a few hypnotic passes and you went sound to sleep.*

Reading this decades-old letter, I was hoping that I'd find some insight into my grandpa. Maybe understand my dad too. I was worried about what kind of father I will be to Zed and Maude. The letter taunts my ambitions. *Have you ever stood so close to an object that you inappropriately described it.* I noticed that he didn't write it as a question.

Sarah

Sarah and I met downtown where the hippies, goths, metalheads and skaters hung out at a coffee shop called Monique's with poetry readings, live bands and an elderly French owner who was relaxed about fifteen-year-olds drinking. With Robert Smith posters on her wall and dyed-red hair, Sarah was on the goth end of the spectrum. I was somewhere between metalhead and hippy, a Florida boy. She and her friends wore skater shoes, baggy jeans and tight T-shirts. There is a photo of her from that time posing on a sea wall. I recognise the place: it is on the north end of the barrier island, Siesta Key, where I lived. Her hands are on her hips. Her smile is wide, and her eyes are shining. The setting sun colours the scene in oranges and reds. Her baggy jeans in the photo are overalls splattered with paint from art class. She still wears them. Her hair is bobbed and fringed. And, that smile! Her eyes sparkle. It is the smile of when she is truly happy. The teenage her and young woman her and the middle-aged mother her are there in that smile. The smile that will haunt me when she is gone.

Back in high school, she smoked Camels, drove a sun-bleached blue Geo Storm and worked as a waitress in a retirement home next to the one I was fired from.

The car was a gift from one of the residents. The most a resident offered me was when I was collecting room service trays and an old man, naked, balls hanging like the wattles of a rooster, invited me into his room offering to take care of me. I politely declined, horrified by the foreknowledge of what gravity and time had planned for my gonads.

I grew up in Florida, and so did my parents and most of my dad's side of the family. Sarah grew up in Europe. Her dad was in the Air Force, and they lived in Taiwan, Crete, Italy and Germany. The most I had seen of the world was on a spontaneous road trip to Atlanta at sixteen, where I had to call my mom so she could tell the front desk clerk to rent me a room for the night. Sarah had recently moved from a New England suburban idyll, complete with a shaggy Old English sheepdog and a father having an affair. After her parents divorced, her mom moved the kids to Florida where the dog lost its hair to the climate and a flea allergy. Instead of family nights at Pizza Man, she was in a Kenny Roger's Roasters dosing her mac and cheese with liquid acid.

During our senior year, our high school organised a photographer to take our pictures for the yearbook. Her maiden name being alphabetically proximate to mine, I was behind her in line. She was there with her mom. Sarah and I got our photos, and we went our own ways. Once I was out of earshot, Sarah's mom, my future mother-in-law, suggested I was a nice young man. To which Sarah agreed. Handsome, too, her mom suggested. If he cut his hair, retorted Sarah.

We didn't date in high school. I had a girlfriend. She had a boyfriend: a tall, skinny, dark-haired boy. My wife definitely has a type. We were friends and that was it and that was enough. After our first night together, years later, when she told her friend, now godmother to our twins, she was incredulous: Jarred, Jarred McGinnis?

The summer before we all drifted away to college, we were hanging out together more often. My best friend was trying to sleep with her. Instead, she had him run errands and I would tag along. Then, she moved to Pittsburgh and I to Houston. That should have been the end of this story. There is no meant to be.

I didn't remember who got in touch first, but Sarah has a better memory and proof. As we manage our daughters and the breakfast routine, she hands me the box of her keepsakes. She tries to tease me about not keeping her letters and I remind her my apartment was cleared out after my accident and I lost correspondence, clothes and a beloved Alvarez acoustic guitar I had had since I was sixteen.

Here's a photo of my aunt's dog in my pants and some stamps. So now you have to send me those letters or come up with a different excuse . . . Enjoy!

Do you know when you're leaving for Christmas? I have so much to say to you. It's easier if I draw it.

On the back, I had drawn a collage of doodles, each labelled in my left-handed chicken scratch and irregular capitalisation: *Flying Ovums (not mine), my amputated TOE, mistake – ignore* and below a pair of buttocks with the words *Sarah is a babe* encircled by a heart, the label read *My new tattoo*. I was clearly flirting. A boy doesn't just mention ova, right?

That Christmas break, a group of us returning from college met up at a Mexican restaurant with fake adobe walls and decorative sombreros. I had brought a Ziplock of random pills that a friend had given me before I left Texas. I had already eaten the shapes I knew: the round blue Valium 10s, the segmented bricks of Xanax. I traded the Ativan for weed. I was left with a pharmaceutical trail mix and had been trying them out, gauging their effects. The big fat whites had the slow soppiness of an opioid. The little brown BBs were extremely unpleasant if you smoked pot. At dinner, I offered Sarah a lucky dip from my baggie.

What's this one? she asked.

Haven't tried one of those yet, I said. She popped the mystery pill and washed it down with a gulp of frozen strawberry margarita. After dinner, we went our separate ways. I remember thinking, I hope I didn't just kill that Sarah girl.

Later that week, when we met up, she teased me that I had been getting high on a bag of allergy medication. We went to a house party together and spent most of the party melting into the same loveseat, watching the antics around us. I had brought a bottle of Wild Irish Rose, a wine I liked for its cheapness and the bowery bum connotations.

I got to go pee, she said. She stood and fought the wobble of the hobo wine, which sneaks up on the couch-bound. She pointed at a pair of green Docs that someone had left beside our couch. Those are nice, she said and walked towards the bathroom.

At the end of the night, we piled into the car and drove off. I surprised her with the green Docs. I pretended it was a coincidence and that I would never steal shoes from a party and then stash them in the car while she was in the bathroom. Inside one of the shoes was forty dollars and a lighter, which I pretended was also part of my gift and remarked on the boundlessness of my generosity. She treated me to Denny's. She got chicken fingers. I had my usual late night meal of coffee and grits. The earlier 'ovum' letter suggests that I already had feelings for Sarah, but I remember the hobo wine and shoe theft Christmas as when I fell for her. She remembers it as the Christmas that I bragged about dating an older woman and her telling me the story of her conversation with her mom about me and my long hair.

In her box of keepsakes, I find a postcard postmarked a month later. It shows a painting of a boy with short hair in a KISS shirt. On the back I wrote, *I wanted to show you what my new haircut looks like. I'm not kidding. Love, Jarred.*

The next Christmas break, we both returned to Florida to see our mothers. On the way I stopped to see my great-grandparents, Bill and Flo. Grandma Flo of the small magic, visited by ghosts. The exit for their house was an American barn painted blue instead of red advertising MERAMEC CAVERNS. The owner falsely claimed that the caverns were used by Jesse James's gang as a hideout and invited a fellow huckster to live on the property and pretend to be the outlaw himself. A court order and later DNA evidence debunked the men's claims, but Grandma Flo retold those hideout stories and said she knew some of the gang's families that lived nearby. Once off the highway, I drove straight until I saw the McGinnis Sho-me Courts sign that still sat in front of their house.

A 1950s-nostalgia website has several photochrome postcards for 'McGinnis Sho-me Courts' diner and motel before the business failed, and they converted the building into their home. The two large windows on either side of the entrance matched my memory. I remember it being skirted with oleanders but none of the images support that recollection. Those trees fruited an inexhaustible crop of orange caterpillars with black whiskers, and black-purple moths that sat on the bare branches watching their brood strip the tree of its leaves. With shining, white-spotted wings and the tips of their abdomens the same orange as the caterpillars, they felt too exotic for the American Midwest's unrelenting greens and browns. As a child, I terrorised those poor creatures. My clothes were smeared in their fluorescent guts.

An online map shows that, seventy years after those postcards, a slow tidal wave of cottonwoods, redbuds and sycamores have risen high above the cement and flat-roofed former diner. By the time I was born, the trees had already claimed the motel: the packed gravel parking lot resisted the encroachment, but the buildings had been demolished. I imagine, in a few more decades, the forest will crash down and consume the house before pushing against the interstate.

Satellite photos still show the quarry Grandpa Bill made with dynamite he had 'acquired' from the road crews building the interstate that drew away the customers from his diner. He said it was his due. He was trying to blow open a new entrance to the nearby Meramec caverns, dreaming of postcards proclaiming: MCGINNIS CAVERNS, SEE SPECTACULAR NATURAL WONDERS. The family story goes that, once the aging explosives started to sweat nitroglycerine, after a near miss, and a worried call from Grandma Flo, my grandpa, as the oldest son, drove up from Florida to confront his dad and confiscate the remaining unstable dynamite. Instead, the men agreed to detonate the leftovers in one last attempt, which attracted law enforcement and feigned ignorance from my elders.

Beside the house, the largest tree is a cottonwood where a tractor tyre was hung for me and visiting cousins to swing on. Before you climbed into the swing, the stagnant water with its cache of squiggling mosquito larvae had to be poured out. The supreme effort required to lift the tyre was part of the fun. In early summer, the fuzz of seeds drifted on the meagre midwestern breeze, and it was the closest a Florida kid like me came to seeing snow. I loved kicking through drifts collecting against the house and coating the yard.

For some reason we never used the front door, and muscle memory led me to the back where Grandma Flo was always waiting at the screen door. She was half as tall as me. She was wearing a white cotton shirt and bright blue trousers that suited her puff of red hair, perfectly done, and matching her lipstick. I imagined if I hugged her too hard, she would turn to cottonwood seed and drift from my arms.

Give your grandma a kiss, you want some coffee? she asked.

We settled down at the kitchen table and I asked where Grandpa Bill was.

Out fussing or fixing, she said.

We sat there and I'm sure she asked about my school, my mom, a life already far removed from hers where she hadn't gone much farther than the county border. Maybe this was the time she told me that the milk from figs can cure warts or talked about my great-great-grandpa, a mallet-fisted local boxing champ whose nickname was Bull McGinnis. He had a gouge in his skull from a childhood accident involving an axe. In his last years, he lived with them. His hair was still black but had thinned with age; his teeth on one side had worn down to the gums from the ever-present pipe. The sweetness of pipe smoke always entered the room moments before he did. He had held on to very little in life beyond a government-issued donkey from his work as a county recorder. When the bars in the nearest town closed, the owner set him on his donkey and the animal knew the way home without needing direction from its slumped passenger. By the time he got back to the house, he had sobered enough to herald his return with a long loud, *who-whee* and a few verses of 'Diddley Doo'. Dutifully, Grandma Flo eased him to bed with his boots still on. I never met Bull McGinnis, but Grandpa Bill had that same who-whee and song.

The story Grandma Flo never told me was that when she was five, her mother died. That on the day of the wake, it was the smell of boiled cabbage she remembered most. This wasn't unusual because often there was nothing else to eat but cabbage. The clothes were hung to dry in the kitchen and that smell was baked into everything the family wore. Cabbage reminded Grandma Flo of being hungry, being cold. She hated cabbage. It clung to the memories of her mother laid on the kitchen table below the clothes racks. Her mother's hands were folded under her arms to hide where she had been burned from a childhood accident. It was said that she had always been embarrassed by the scars. Grandma Flo would have explained that the dead too have their pride. With her arms folded across her chest, it looked like her mother, who was leaving five orphans including a ten-month-old baby brother, was disappointed with how it all turned out. I can hear Grandma Flo's voice pronouncing, there's no shame in being poor, but there's not much pleasure in it either. She never told me how her childhood was spent unwanted and eventually as an indentured servant to a wealthy St. Louis family until she met my great-grandpa Bill at sixteen who seemed a better bet than her current circumstances.

Perhaps I was told but didn't listen. It's a story that I have caught whispers of as my grandfather's siblings made sense of their childhood. Their stories don't have the tint of nostalgia that my stories of great-grandpa Bill have. When they were kids, he too was a drunk. Hyper-critical and dismissive of his children. He spent the meagre household money in the same bars that killed his father while his children waited outside, never daring to go in. The other story that Grandma Flo would never have told me was that after a particular night of drunken violence, she had had enough. She went down to the stream to pick Jack-in-the-pulpit, though she would have called them Indian turnips. Eaten raw, it causes horrific nausea and vomiting, as well as blistering and swelling severe enough to prevent speaking. The Meskwaki knew this plant. In battle, they would feign a rout, leaving food adulterated with the plant. The ravenous American soldiers, not having read their Xenophon, would eat the meat and be thankful when the Meskwaki returned to put them out of their misery with a rifle butt to the head.

As a rural child of the depression, Grandma Flo would have known this famine food. The tubers are edible when cooked and add a peppery flavour to otherwise bland frontier cuisine. She put a few uncooked slices into Grandpa Bill's stew and, as he lay on the bathroom floor, she stood over him and said, Never again. They never divorced or separated, and I like to hope that it was indeed never again.

While we were chatting, Grandpa Bill appeared on the front step, gripping his thumb tight against his chest.

His beer gut suited his broad shoulders. Regardless of the weather, he wore a white undershirt and blue jeans. The only thing that varied was the brand name on the front of his baseball cap. That day's read, CAT DIESEL POWER. He might have been an intimidating man but, when he tilted his head back to look through his bifocals, his green eyes magnified comically.

He shouted through the screen door, Momma? Bring me your sewing kit?

A delta of blood flowed between his fingers and down his arm.

What'd you want with my sewing kit? Grandma Flo asked.

Quit your fussing. Bring me a needle and some thread. He turned to me and said, going to need your help here.

I stared at the drops of blood that left his elbow and dotted his shirt. His tendons were taut against the thick freckled flesh of his arms.

When Grandma Flo saw the blood, she chorused, Oh

my goodness, what have you done now, what happened, what'd you do, oh my goodness.

I felt a lurch of queasiness as I stepped outside.

I'll be all right. That needle threaded? he asked his wife. And fetch some rubbing alcohol, will you? Thank you.

I sat beside him on a bench. My vision went green as he asked me to hold the torn flesh of his thumb while he stitched, with sky-blue thread, the gash that ran from the tip of the digit to the meat of his palm. He pushed the needle through the yellowed callused skin then drew the thread to bring the edges together and hide the thin line of fatty curds. He must have noticed the colour leaving my face. His slow, deep voice like truck wheels on gravel asked, You all right, boy? which kept me from passing out.

Stay with me now. We're almost done here, he said. His skin was sticky with drying blood. I adjusted my grip, and the cut reopened with a fresh dollop of red. Steady, he said.

The copper smell churned acid in my stomach. Grandma Flo approached with a plastic bottle. He nodded to her, pausing his sewing. She poured the clear liquid over our hands as timidly as if she was going to feel the pain. Grandpa Bill closed his eyes. His mouth tightened. He gave a who-whee and stamped his boot a couple of times.

All right. That'll do. Momma, now, we got some clean rags or bandages? Something? After she left, he leaned in and whispered, Let's get this done before that woman comes back and tries to kill me again. He winked. He finished his uneven suture.

Are you okay? I asked.

Me? You're the one green around the gills. Thanks for helping me play doctor.

That night we ate our dinner of homemade fried chicken and mashed potatoes lined up on the couch with TV trays in front of us like game show contestants. Grandpa Bill ignored our concerns for the injury wrapped in pale cream rags, but I couldn't stop thinking about the vivid wound hidden beneath.

When the eerie tremolo of a screech owl came in through the screen door, Grandpa Bill said, Don't worry, he ain't calling for me. I'm too pretty to die. In the Southern tradition, hearing a screech owl's call three times meant there would be a death in the family.

He asked me what I was studying at college. I told him philosophy.

He shouted Who-wee, what the heck you going to do with that? You want to hear how I met your great-grandma. It was in church.

Don't you dare, Grandma Flo warned and stood to take our trays into the kitchen. His grin stretched full of mischief.

That's right, I met her in church. She was chasing me though. Well, she caught me all right. She chased me and chased me until she caught me by the organ. The preacher blushed beet red when he saw her do it. I'm telling you.

I shook my head as his laugh rumbled from his belly.

She's been in love with me ever since.

*

My bed for the night was the couch in the front room. In my dream I saw two sisters. The taller one wore a double strand of pearls tight against her throat and her right wrist. They wore matching fur-collared coats. Their teeth were too big for their mouths as they smiled. My attention was drawn to the couch I was sleeping on, but it was empty. Later, after emailing family for photos, I figured out that these women were the owners of the family graveyard. The place where my great-grandparents, my grandfather and, eventually, my father are buried.

That visit was the last time I saw either Grandpa Bill or Grandma Flo. I have the typical regrets that I didn't call and visit them enough. That soon I would be dying beneath a truck doesn't mitigate my guilt.

After Christmas day spent with our mothers, Sarah picked me up to go to a house party. Almost immediately after arriving, a mutual friend asked if we wanted to see something fucked up.

Sarah said, I hope it's not a dead body, I didn't bring my poking stick. We were led to a huge bathroom with a jacuzzi tub. A crowd was surrounding an older naked goth woman. As we arrived the crowd jumped back, screamed, laughed, fled, as a frothing jet of red wine sprayed from her ass onto the porcelain and fixtures. The woman howled with relief as the wine continued to gurgle out.

Our friend joked we should try the wine enema.

Sarah shot back, Twice in one night? I couldn't possibly.

It's a shame, I thought. I won't be able to tell our future grandkids that at this exact moment I knew she was the person I could laugh with for the rest of my life.

The goth slumped onto the toilet as two others prepared a dose for a disrobing older man with inch-thick plugs in his ears. We left the party shortly after – what could top goths butt-chugging Manischewitz wine? – and drove to the beach.

On the way Sarah stopped at a convenience store to buy cigarettes while I waited in the car. There was a straw's paper wrapper in the footwell, scrunched and stamped into the shape of an S. That felt significant. I needed everything to be meaningful in case this was the moment we began our life together.

I opened her glove compartment. It was empty. Where does she keep her insurance documentation? Maps? Instruction manual for the car? What about emergency water and food in case she goes off the road, flips over and is trapped for days until the snow melts and then – what will she think when she discovers this boy is a worrier, a self-doubter and not the free spirit he plays at? I picked up the S of straw paper and put it in the glove box. When I tried to shut it, it sprang open again. After a few attempts, worried she'd return to find that I had broken her glovebox, I discovered a baby chick toy was blocking the hinges. A fluff of yellow velveteen glued roughly to a plastic mould with poorly painted black dots for eyes. When you put your finger on two metal circles underneath, it completed a circuit and the chick made tinny electric peeps. I was picking at the seam of its yellow pelt when the head came off. I stuffed it into my pocket chirping its electronic accusations as Sarah returned to the car.

We sat on a beached catamaran and watched the blackness of the sea at night beyond the powdered sugar sand that made the island famous. A dozen Portuguese man-o-wars had washed ashore before us. She listened to my wonder at these turquoise wrecks. Creatures that were not creatures but both vessel and crew. An animal that was actually a colony of thousands of individuals. We went silent admiring these easy miracles.

She asked what I was thinking about.

I honestly answered I was thinking about the goths and how the parents of the person whose house party it was will be confused when they find wine stains on the inside seat of their fancy bathrobes.

She laughed.

I asked, You know that Easter toy in your glove box?

No. What were you doing in my glove box?

It was a little plastic chicken that peeped.

Okay.

Was it important?

I'm not sure. What is it again?

I dug it out of my pocket. She plucked the body and was surprised to see the head didn't follow.

She took the head to set it on top of the body as if that was how easily broken things are fixed. I'll learn soon enough that she has an unshakeable optimism for broken things, and it will save my life. She looked genuinely sad, attempting to fix the toy, making an occasional electric peep when her hands touched the metal circles.

I'm sorry.

What did you do?

He was a traitor to the revolution, I said as I took the head back.

She grabbed for it. I raised my arm taking advantage of my height. She tackled me and I obligingly fell onto the boat as we wrestled for the head. The weight of her against me decades later feels the same as it did then.

We went to a friend's house. We got drunk playing cards and, as the party wound down, we sat together. When our knees touched, neither of us moved our legs away. Then a hand found another. I ran my thumb along the length of her fingers. Back and forth. Soft skin, slender knuckles. She leaned her shoulder against mine and pulled my arm around her. The tips of my fingers traced back and forth the shadow of her collarbone. When it was time to go to bed, her girlfriend offered to share the guest room with Sarah.

Jarred and I can sleep in the guest room, Sarah suggested.

Christmas vacation over, we both went back to our corners of the US, she to Pennsylvania and I to Texas. We made plans for her to visit me in Austin. *I know there are a few perfect sentences I could write to you. Sentences to make you think of me and smile . . . When you get to Texas it will be like we never said goodbye in Florida.*

In trying to reconstruct those months before my accident, I order my letters by postmark. I cringe at the callow ramblings and my overwrought prose. I relive the making and undoing of plans, and see the moments that lead towards the inevitability of my accident. It awakens aches along fractures that I thought healed. In the letters, we agreed a relationship was impossible.

We were honest about dating other people. It was sensible to date others. We were thousands of miles apart, but I was increasingly dissatisfied. I remember stopping at a payphone outside a 7-11, to tell her about a disastrous date. I had gone home with a girl whose house was so filthy that foreplay was interrupted when I choked on a dust bunny. Sarah too was dating. She told me of a painting that a boy had given her. It was of her masturbating and mid-orgasm. I was not jealous of their relationship so much as my inability to paint. She then told me it was getting serious with the painter. *I understand that this letter will not change things and that you already have feelings for someone else.*

When she returned from her trip to Texas, she broke it off with the painter. He was distraught. He wrote similar pleading messages and gave her more paintings. In the box of letters that Sarah has given me to write this part of our lives, I've reached the strata of postmarked envelopes and postcards where our relationship became more solid. She too was talking about love and planning how we could live in the same city, but we were still unsure how.

On the back of a photocopy of Elliott Erwitt's *Boy with Pistol, 1950*, I sent her another letter. The photo is of a young boy holding a pistol to his temple. His face is gap-toothed glee, a manic 'Howdy Doody' look. His eyes sparkle above crab-apple cheeks. He stands against a tree. Braces hold up his two-sizes-too-big jeans, sleeves rolled up against him being swallowed by the shirt he wears. I write about how much I enjoy her teaching me about art, introducing me to Erwitt's work and how I can't wait to go to more museums with her. The letter ends, *Our week doesn't even seem real. It feels like a wish in some dream I had. Now I want to go back to bed and see how it ends because a good dream can't end with goodbyes in a lonely airport.*

I discovered that the University of Pittsburgh has a good philosophy department. I travelled to see her and to speak with a professor about transferring. While I was there, I bought her a bouquet of royal-blue irises from a man selling them at a crosswalk. The irises were the only flowers that looked fresh among the buckets. We still buy each other irises. They have been made significant by those first ones.

When I returned to Austin, I sent her copies of the photos I took during my visit. She laughed that they were mostly images of her basement. I had only ever seen them in movies. A basement is an impossibility in Florida. But then the plan for me to move to Pittsburgh was undone by a scholarship to the University of Texas. It was an opportunity I couldn't miss, and the letters returned to uncertainty. They are heavy, sad letters that I find hard to read even now. *I could never ask you to move if I'm unwilling to do the same.*

The postmarks inch closer to the day of my accident. We were on the verge of calling it off when her friend and coworker decided to move to Austin to go to film school. It pushed her to enrol. They would move down to Texas, and we three would share an apartment near campus. I was meant to drive up to Pittsburgh to help them move down. I had already put down a deposit on a two-bedroom apartment. We'd take our time, make a vacation of it and be in Austin for the first of August.

The day before my twenty-first birthday in July, I was beneath a truck smelling earth and grease and my burning flesh. There was no pain at the time. Pain came later. It was only the sizzling sound of a burger being pressed into the grill by a spatula, the taste of dirt in my mouth, and knowing something very very bad was happening. Occasionally, decades after, exactly like the Hollywood flashback of a war vet, I hear the skin, muscle and fat of my left shoulder cooking away. In front of my eyes the overlaid shadow cutout of the driver's-side wheel and the bright blues and greens of a Texas summer beyond. My truck, which had a faulty emergency brake, had started to roll. I have a thin slice of a memory as I put my hands out to stop it. Then a blackout surge, even decades later, of fear, like when a fuse in the house blows. I'm plunged into a blind panic, and it takes a few moments and deep breaths to recover. Surprisingly often strangers ask, What happened to you? as if I owe them an explanation for my disabled body. My daughters too have asked. I have never been able to tell them the story. The density of suffering created that day still has a gravity I cannot deny. To conjure the moment is to bring myself pain. I don't owe anyone my pain, not even my daughters. It feels like I'm hiding something from them, but it is to keep it from myself.

The other sliver of memory is that I hear sirens. I know they are coming for me. A fireman is talking to me in a calm voice. I too am calm. I am found. Then nothing. Medical reports detail severe traumas, loss of blood, an ambulance ride and unconsciousness. The only person unaware I would never walk again. My memories from those first weeks are poorly lit impressions, seared scenes and total blackouts. The first time I regained consciousness I knew I was in a hospital, but the colours of the world were wrong. The room's angles were exaggeratedly acute like in my dreams of the dead and their homes. The fluorescent lighting above hummed a malevolent orange-black. I was aware of a great danger. The nurses skulking on the other side of the curtain were a coven of man-hating lesbian witches experimenting on me. That was obvious.

ICU delirium occurs in up to 70 per cent of patients admitted into acute care. This hyperactive psychosis, an unfortunate and outdated misnomer for what I was experiencing, came from the shock of the accident swizzled with the chemical trauma from the medications used to save my life. I felt at my face. They had sewn an ear where my nose should have been. I had to escape. What devious sapphic machinations necessitated sewing an ear to a man's nose? I worried at the artificial ear. The stitches came loose with a wet ripping sound. I tried to examine it through the blurred clouds of colour. I had pulled out the intubation tube. Warm black liquid poured over my face. That wasn't a hallucination. That was my stomach contents. A nurse came in, a coven member I suspected, but the fear and shock on her face made me think that the witches hadn't got to her yet and she was a regular nurse. I tried to warn her, to get her to help me escape. I felt relief as my bed whipped through the hospital, watching endless double doors flying open before us, as the coven closed in.

When I came to, I was still in the same hospital room, but my hands had been strapped down. Eventually the hallucinations ceased, and I spent long days waiting for the surgeon who saved my life to check on me and most importantly top up the morphine. Besides her medical acumen, she radiated care and peace. I felt safe with her. She lent me her MP3 player, it had more Whitney Houston than I was used to, but it was better than hearing the wet gurgle from the bullet wound in the face of the patient beside me. Across the room an INS officer stood in front of a small room isolating one patient from the others. The man in the bed couldn't be seen for equipment, tubing, bandages and pillows. He was reduced to a crest of black hair above a field of white and hospital light blue. He had been hit by a train trying to cross the border and the officer was there to escort him to Mexico once he had stabilised. It was a room of suffering, and I belonged. I disappeared into strange opioid dreams of faceless men and loose-wigged cyborgs soundtracked by 'Didn't We Almost Have It All'.

When I thought about Sarah, it was to mourn our

relationship. That was over. My life was over. Everything we had been planning together was cancelled. The apartment I found for us, which was up two flights of stairs, was being emptied by my family and they were arguing with the landlord to get my deposit back. At the time I wasn't being moved out of bed, so the understanding of disability hadn't arrived yet. I was still supposed to be thankful that I was alive despite the spinal cord injury and the paraplegia. I had skin grafts on my back from where the engine block pinned me under the truck. My legs were cast to my thighs with multiple fractures. I would learn later that the orthopaedic surgeon hadn't bothered to set my foot facing the correct direction because 'I wouldn't be using it anyway'.

Once my brain had dried out from the cocktail of medications and the hospital had been cleared of occultists, a friend visited me. I was coherent enough to tell him Sarah's number.

Can you call her and let her know what happened? I don't know if she knows yet.

He couldn't disguise his look of horror, and I wasn't sure he was listening as he stared and nodded. He made a few attempts at small talk. I waited for him to make his excuses and leave me alone with this new shame I felt.

I ask Sarah about this time in our lives. She remembers the phone call from my friend. He, like everyone else, thought I was going to die and urged her to come as fast as she could. It wasn't possible for non-family to visit me in ICU. She was not family then and it made more sense to wait until I had been moved to a long-term rehabilitation hospital in Houston before she drove the thousand miles to visit me.

She remembers being unsure what she was going to do. She considered moving back to Florida or staying in Pittsburgh. She didn't know. At the time, it was another sadness in my life that was so stuffed full of them that we didn't talk about it. Instead, while I picked at my hospital tray of a meat, a boiled vegetable or two, a cup of iridescent canned fruit and a small blue milk carton like the ones I remember from elementary school lunchrooms, she phoned to tell me about her road trip. As she made her way to Texas, we discussed the change of landscape as the openness of the Midwest and its palette of browns were swallowed by the South's tangle of greens.

She was staying with her friend's grandparents in Louisiana for a few days. Two adorable backcountry folk who, for more than a half-century, had made a home with a screened-in porch and a Cadillac in the driveway. She told me about how their door was never locked and about the rotation of neighbours and friends stopping by to sit for a cup of coffee at the huge table in the kitchen, the sound of *M*A*S*H* coming from the TV in the front room. She was charmed by their Southern hospitality, constant offers of sweet tea and too much food. She boasted about her first experience of sucking crawdad heads.

My days were the hospital's bland landscape of function and routine. A purgatory between the life I had lived as an able-bodied young man and the life in a wheelchair that I couldn't see as being possible. In constant pain, I couldn't sit up for more than an hour. The details of my day were quickly skipped over with a 'fine'.

My mom was sitting at my bedside. She had flown in from Florida and was staying with her sister. We were watching the small TV hanging above us. Princess Diana had died in a car accident, the only tragedy that mattered. The news camera panned across the London crowds as they left flowers. We watched the gates of Buckingham Palace leaning under the weight of the bouquets and posters with Diana's face and bubble-lettered messages. A small child in the background was retching from the stench of thousands of lilies. We love you, People's Princess. The video cut to the police growing impatient with the crowd as it pushed in. We lip-read their 'stay back stay back' but the sound was lost amongst the crying and shouting of the agitated crowd. The gate slowly bowed with a metallic moan, and we watched impassively. The camera cut to people queueing to push through the palace's wicket gate as the commentator, a grey-haired Englishman, gave a calm RP description of the rioting and looting. An elderly woman triumphantly waved a torn piece of bed linen with the Windsor crest for the camera while jerking it away from the grasping hands around her. My bedside phone rang. Sarah was downstairs.

Could I come up and see you? she asked.

Of course.

My stomach fluttered to hear her voice, to have her close again. She walked through the hall between large framed portraits of rigid old men in doctor's whites. Her friend asked if he should come up with her. Sarah said no and came to my room alone. When she is shy, she puts on a small tight smile and looks at you side-eyed. She did that then and our daughters do the same thing now when we tell them to say hello to adults who stand so tall above them, smiling too broadly, saying incomprehensible things. My mom introduced herself as Momo, which was a childhood nickname given to her by her younger sister. When she married my dad, the McGinnises adopted the name too. My daughters call her Momo. The world is full of grandmas, grannies, nans and even meemaws. I like that my daughters have something unique, a Momo.

After pleasantries were exchanged, I asked Momo to give us a moment alone. I pretended not to see her face fall and her feelings hurt. Her only son, and I wanted Sarah, not her, to be beside me.

Sarah and I held each other. She frowned as she touched the lingering green crescent of my black eye that remained long after the accident. My arms were still cross-hatched in scabs. We kissed, she leaning into the hospital bed. The smell, taste, feel, the reality of her was the first moment after the accident that I was more than an absence. I had been reduced to the tally of what I had lost. The thought that I could live a normal life was impossible. The irony is that the decades of being disabled has taught me that the hardest part is having interactions with able-bodied people who have the same presumption. I tend to be overtly rude to people who bring the same ignorance I once had. It's no surprise that the borders of shame and anger are shared.

Still in hospital gowns and in constant pain, a new self would be reconstituted. It would take years, but it was now possible. The taste of Sarah's lips, breathing in her scent, were the edge pieces of that puzzle. Without her I know, not suspect, that I would not have survived the injuries I sustained. Through the physical recovery, as my understanding of self was reforming, I never doubted that I was loved. Without Sarah, that would have been impossible to believe.

She showed me a pair of shorts and a shirt she had bought me for my birthday. The birthday I spent unconscious as surgeons sawed away a piece of my hipbone to serve as an ersatz vertebra. I haven't worn shorts since my accident. I'm too self-conscious of the atrophied gnarls of bone and skin below my waist. As I opened her gifts, I paused. I fought the heat and tears. I switched off the TV as a reporter in a bright blue dress stood on the crumpled bonnet of Prince Charles's Mercedes outside of St James's Palace.

I told Sarah, you don't have to be here. I don't want to be here, but I have to. You don't have to be here. If you left now, I wouldn't blame you.

If either of my daughters came to me in Sarah's situation, even today after all we have together, I would have said, Leave him. That boy is cute and all but don't be charmed by his humour and excellent parking options.

Sarah was unsure throughout the whole drive down to Texas whether she wanted this. Watching East Texas's curtain of forest blur by, she composed her 'Dear John'. She was twenty-one years old. Did it make sense to make a lifetime commitment to a boy she had been dating for barely six months? Most of our relationship had been calls from pay phones late at night. She in Pittsburgh, and I in Austin. Her mom had spoken her doubts, trying to convince her to avoid this youthful folly, however well intentioned. There is no meant to be.

Below the bowl of my skull, the X-rays showed an orderly architecture of spine. Each square of intact bone meant my life was a little less worse. Had the construction here failed, I wouldn't be able to move my arms, hands, fingers or breathe unaided. As the nurse explained this, my first thought was, At least I could kill myself, and that desperate thought was a comfort. Immediately below were the twelve thoracic vertebrae. These too were uninjured, which meant I avoided a susceptibility to pneumonia, immunodeficiencies, and a particular cruel horror, almost unique to spinal cord injuries, called autonomic dysreflexia where your autonomic nervous system short circuits. I remember seeing a fellow patient have an attack as the hidden controls of himself sought rebellion. He was sweating profusely as he screamed about his head, pulling at his chest as if he wanted his skin off.

Though my spinal cord was intact here, in the X-ray, the grey shadows of bone were flanked by a dual violence of bright white. These were two rods of titanium hardware with screws unevenly distributed, spoiling the symmetry of the image. Their visible threads amassed below the first, second and third lumbar vertebrae, where the spine had turned to the chewed-up remnants of something fine. The injury was incomplete, which meant, for all the miracles of modern medicine, I was prescribed eighteen months of wait and see. Wait and see could mean complete functional recovery or wait and see could mean nothing at all.

The key was to avoid further damage. I was fitted with a clamshell brace, so I looked like a bleached ninja turtle whose martial-art speciality was zero range of motion. When orthopaedics had made the casts, I was still emaciated from my time spent in acute care. The brace became more painful as I regained weight, but I had to wear it to give my bones time to fuse with the rods. Every morning it was a two-orderly procedure to get me into the hospital's wheelchair. With my right leg still in a full cast and jutting before me like the ramming prow of a cursed ship, I made my slow progress to the physical therapy room.

The therapists were mostly middle-aged women. The patients, mostly young men, broken by bad luck or stupidity. I couldn't stand pedalling away at a hand cycle or being strapped to a tilt table like Frankenstein's monster to see if my blood pressure could handle forty-five degrees after so many weeks horizontal in bed. That these things were important to recover a mote of all that I had lost didn't matter. I turned the chair and pointed my broken leg towards the exit with no plan but to escape. I enjoyed the weighted blanket of heat after so long in the dry hospital AC. The sidewalks were wide and flat and untroublesome for my ungainly barque.

At the back of the hospital, the sidewalk sloped into the driveway where the ambulances brought the newest patients. In my memory, it was an impossibly steep grade, but an online street view shows a gentle dip that today I wouldn't even notice. I tried to navigate the slope, but lost control and slid towards the road. As the front casters fell off the sidewalk, I lurched forward and felt a pain in my spine that the shell did not save me from. If I fell out of this chair onto the road, my spine would break at the screws and those meagre abilities like breathing would be taken away too. I would shatter. The street sweeper pulling along his cart would pause to sigh at the pieces of me before pulling out his broom and dustpan. He would right the wheelchair and push it back to the storeroom for the next occupant of my bed.

I tried pulling myself back from this precipice of inches, but it was beyond my ability. I had to rock the chair back and forth and each time I felt my body, fixed by the brace, teeter, ready to fall from the chair. I finally managed enough momentum to bring the castors back onto the sidewalk and retreated into the hospital. The shock of the AC made me realise I was soaked in sweat. I went back to my room, stopping at the nurse's station to ask them to help me into bed. I didn't leave the hospital again until I was discharged.

The orthopaedic surgeon at the rehab hospital recast the leg so that my foot pointed in the right direction. It would heal. But the burn on my shoulder was a concern. The flesh was burned to the bone. I had no idea that it was sepsis, more than anything, that was likely to kill me. Each morning, when the nurse changed the bandage, its yellow and pinkish stain was examined for auguries of my discharge date. As the spot on the gauze shrank, my fear grew. Death didn't make me realise the preciousness of life: no diems were carped. Nor did my intimacy with death make me more afraid of it. It was the living that scared me now. Beyond the automatic doors of the hospital, shame awaited. No one taught me that the disabled body was a failure, but it was a lesson I had learned. Even now, the truth of it nips.

Above the floor where we, the newly damaged, laid our fragile forms on blue egg-crate mattresses, was a secure unit for long-term residents. When I suggested I wasn't ready to leave the hospital, I don't remember anyone arguing. The physical therapist wheeled me to the secure unit floor to see the facilities. She showed me the beds. Four to a room. Indistinguishable from my current set-up. In the day room was a family sitting at a table. All of them looked exhausted as they sipped at their coffees or stared into their cups. The mom sat beside her teenage daughter and talked to her. The daughter was beautiful, maybe a year or two younger than me. The only visible sign that she belonged in the unit was the helmet. It seemed a medieval punishment, a scold's bridle upon an innocent. As the physical therapist recited the details about the vending machine and visitor policies, I watched the girl and her family. Her eyes revealed unseen damage. She was not looking at the same room as the rest of us.

An animal howl made us jump. The girl threw her face to the table. All the cups were upset and the family moved with a fire crew's synchronisation. The mom, tears in her eyes, and the dad with a blank expression restrained their daughter, repeating words of calm. The siblings and aunts fanned out to get paper towels and sop up the spill racing to the table's edge as the girl fitted in her mom's arms. The attack passed, and the girl's eyes returned to the staring emptiness of before. The family settled back into their positions around her. One auntie was still chasing the last dribbles with a wad of paper towel, and the brother and sister stared at the broken stranger in their sister's body. Following the physical therapist back to my room, I was ashamed of my cowardice. Even in the wheelchair with a back brace and a leg cast, I thought, my problem was that I had no problems. I began arrangements for my discharge.

My aunt and uncle lived near the rehab hospital in Clear Lake City. It's a grid of houses on the edge of Houston best known for being the place that astronauts address as 'Houston' as in 'Houston, we have a problem.' 'Clear Lake City, we did an oopsie,' isn't what you want to hear when space trouble is brewing. The roads through the grid were wide enough for two lanes of traffic each way but not a single sidewalk, and it was a twenty-minute walk to reach the vast seas of strip-mall parking lots that surrounded the neighbourhood. The house had no windows, only skylights, because the previous owners were NASA chimpanzee scientists and swingers. My aunt and uncle removed the erotic wallpaper from everywhere but the closets. It was always a small surprise to pull out a coat and glimpse a watercolour orgy of chubby ladies and top-hatted men.

The chimpanzees had lived in what became my aunt's sewing room. The floors sloped to where the drain used to be so that dropped pins or buttons reliably rolled towards the centre of the room.

Years later, Sarah admitted that on her first sight of me in the hospital bed, shocked by how thin I had become, all the Dear Johns she had been composing no longer made sense. She would stay with me. In all our apartments over the decades we've been together, she has collected the battered and abused plants that others have thrown out. As they drop their last pitiful yellow leaves, I ask if I can give them an honourable death in the compost heap, but Sarah persists. She crows when she saves them and mourns when she cannot. Maybe I was just her first trash-heap orchid. There is no meant to be but the love I've known has made it hard to believe that.

As I was in a loaned wheelchair and my right leg cast over the knee, getting in and out of the car took effort, very little of it mine. Sarah had to lift me, with my arms draped over her shoulder, into the car. She had to lift each insensate leg into the footwell of her Geo Storm. There I would sit useless as she disassembled the wheelchair, too big and too heavy for the constant use of a paraplegic. She took me to my appointments and there were so many. Repeating the procedure every time. But it was a time of just us. Long car rides through the infinity of roads and endless traffic that is Houston, Texas, where we talked, continuing those long phone calls started when we were a thousand miles apart. At my physical-therapy appointments, they played anaemic country songs. 'Still the One' by Shania Twain was on heavy rotation. It is an inarguably vapid tune, but it is our song, and it wells the emotions I have for Sarah every time I play it as a joke.

That first chair, loaned by the hospital, was a burden to me, and to others. First chairs are inevitably too wide or too short. Swing-away footplates are good for those who can take an uncertain step or two but, for me, it was extra weight and yet another brittle mechanism to fail. Eventually, a bespoke chair would be made for me. Lighter, easier to take apart, and sturdier.

I'm on my sixth bespoke chair. Each time I've tweaked the configuration to better conform to my needs. The first time your thumb gets stuck between the wheel and the brake and pulls off your nail, you realise the wisdom of brakes that fold away and under the chair. Once the seat angle wasn't quite right which meant I had back pain for five years until insurance deemed that I was eligible for a new one. When I lay down, the remnants of my lower back would click into place like a door with a stiff latch. I removed the handles early on because too many people push you without asking. Imagine someone grabbing you by the shoulders, because you weren't crossing the street fast enough.

The mass of the wheelchair is the most important consideration. I go for as light as possible because a chair's weight is volatile. There are days in which it dissipates. I fly to the tops of hills, pop into trains, travel in seaplanes and there is only the faintest hint of the chair as I do. Then there are days I feel its heaviness on every incline. These attacks of gravity come with no warning. I cannot pin them to my moods or season. In these moments, the seat presses at my hips. The wheels chafe against calluses until they crack and bleed. The bearings grind against grit and casters snag on the smallest pebble. On these days, when a passerby asks if I need help, I give a nod of assent and say thanks. Soon others notice our struggle and grab a part of the chair to push or tug it forward. Despite the pain in my legs and the weakness in my arms, I feel a special hope for humanity's kindness. An elderly neighbour hands off her shopping trolley and climbs into my lap to pilot us around the cracks and tree roots. By the time we reach the apartment, a crowd of people are helping me with the key in the door, ensuring I don't roll back, holding my backpack, moving the door mat out of the way and picking the mail off the floor. The greengrocer and his entire family lift me into bed. His teenage sons that help on the weekends take a leg each in perfect coordination. They even remove my shoes; though unasked for, it's appreciated. The crowd nod and slap each other's backs. They chatter about what we've done here today. They shout best wishes to me as they let themselves out. My smile follows their departure, and I take a rest. A reset. Knowing that after an hour or so the chair's weight will have become more stable. The caprice of Earth's gravity will have moved onto some other poor schmuck.

Disabled or not, the only legal activities in Clear Lake City are to shop or eat. Sarah and I risk fines for anti-consumerism by taking walks. These walks were not intentionally about building my strength, but it was a nice consequence. Mostly the time was perfecting our being together. We stood before houses in the neighbourhood, pretending they were ours. We discussed the merits and deficiencies of our new home. We daydreamed of a time I would be healed enough for us to live on our own. The centrepiece of this fantasy was to have a cat. On our walks up and down the rows and columns of wide empty streets, we invented a game of 'counting cats'. We knew which houses had reliably friendly animals and would aim our wanderings past those. On windy late-autumn days, perfect cat weather, one house on our route could be relied upon to add as many as five calicos to our scores. Over time, I was strong enough to push to a small doughnut shop where we would celebrate with a coffee and a glazed.

Besides caring for me, Sarah took a job as a waitress at a 'down home' Texan-themed restaurant. One night, she called to say she was getting a drink with her coworkers after her shift. She wouldn't be out late; would I be okay?

I'll be okay. I've got the monitor.

For the times when Sarah was at work, my aunt and uncle had bought a baby monitor in case I needed anything. The unit in my room was blue for boys with a single stubby arm reaching upward to send my calls for help.

But Sarah didn't come home. She didn't message. By two, the bars and clubs would have been closed. When I heard her car pull into the driveway, I felt foolish for thinking all the terrible things that could have happened. I waited for her in our bed with the skylight above me framing the moon.

But she didn't come into the house.

A panic built up a pressure in me until I had to get out of bed. I had to do something. I no longer needed the back brace and the cast had been cut down to a half-leg but getting myself out of bed still required assistance. I managed it by using the momentum of dropping my legs over the side. I moved through the dark house, careful not to mash my unfeeling toes or catch them on a corner. Her car was in the driveway, but she wasn't in it. I looked around, panicked, for an explanation. I went back into the house and found her passed out on the couch.

In the morning, she was all apologies against my anger. She and her coworkers went to a terrible club in a strip mall. She drank too much, too quickly. She had passed out in her car in the parking lot, too drunk to drive. She was twenty-one and caring for a paraplegic. She wanted a night of being twenty-one and irresponsible. I understand that now.

*

I think I should go home for Christmas, Sarah said.

Okay, good idea, I said, but anticipated my loneliness and helplessness without her. Each night neuropathic pain, my 'crazy pain', either at my hips, my back or my legs awoke me with their confused messages of agony. Each time I hesitated to wake her, but inevitably I did and she, still half-asleep, rolled me over, repositioning the pillows between the driftwood of my knees. We spent a lot of time in that bed with the skylight above us. I hurt less there.

Can I use the truck? she asked. I don't think the Storm will make it.

I had managed to run myself over. The truck that had destroyed my life because of a faulty emergency brake still sat in my aunt and uncle's driveway. I don't remember that bothering me, but I also don't remember ever getting inside or close to it again.

Of course, I said.

I want to spend Christmas with my mom and sisters, she said as if she needed to explain herself. And Momo will be here. You should spend some time with your mom.

I understood that it was hard to be a stranger among my family. To feel like a guest when you wanted to feel at home had a cost.

I'll be okay, I said. She needed a break from the constant giving of herself that I required. The days of my many appointments. The nights of being woken up so that she could help me. The mornings when a nurse armed with a suppository and a gloved finger arrived and Sarah, my girlfriend of six months, excused herself from the room.

With Sarah away, a living stone settled in my chest. I felt its blackish-green mica-flecked threads following the curve of my ribs to encircle my lungs until some mornings I fought for breath. Along its veins, it whispered all the terrible truths of the disabled body I inhabited. My vision became the colour of stagnant water, and darkness preceded me in any room I entered. Everyone in the house felt the weight of this stone. It was painful for my family to be helpless to repair the fragments of the boy they had known. They wanted me to see a psychiatrist and ideally get medication. In America, sadness is a failure. If you are sad, you've done something wrong.

Since my accident I can control my dreams. I let nightmares play on for the same reason people go to horror films, but if I don't like what my brain is playing, I wake myself up or I change the dream to something else. There alone at night beneath the skylight, I could dream the stone in my chest had no weight. I was free. I dreamt of sex with Sarah, with others, with others and Sarah. I had adventure dreams stolen from black-and-white Samurai films that I adore. I delighted in making weird dreams stranger with a turn of the kaleidoscope of my imagination.

Momo only saw the unwashed young man who had been her son. At the time I only wore hospital scrubs. The crazy pain made heavier fabrics feel like my skin was burning. Each morning Mom had to watch me emerge from my bedroom and make a bowl of cereal, never making eye contact, mumbling brief replies before disappearing back to bed and that weightless freedom of sleep.

One day, she managed to get me to play cribbage. She had played cribbage with her mom. There was a pleasure in that continuity that makes it hard to deny Momo's request for a game. It's relatively simple to play if you can add to fifteen. We set up the board with its scoring pegs. I shuffled the cards. Momo and I sat in the dining room counting our hands, pegging the score. She broached the subject of my depression.

I can't look at your head. It's godawful, Momo said.

Sarah had found an old bottle of hair bleach under the bathroom sink and out of boredom we bleached my hair with it. The result was a flame orange. Contrasted with my black and Mediterranean-thick eyebrows, the result, I admit, was unsettling.

I want a red-headed child but not like this, she joked.

It was Momo's crib. In cribbage, you take turns playing an extra hand made from cards discarded by the players. If it's your crib, you try to give yourself point-scoring cards and if it's the other player's you throw away your value-less cards. She broached the subject of talking to someone, getting help, maybe a prescription.

I gave her the two cards for her crib and said, If I can't be sad now, at this, when can I be? She added her two cards. She cried as we did the count. Eight, fifteen for two, twenty-two for two, go, twenty-seven and the one for go. That was the last time we talked about it.

When I spoke to my aunt about this time in my life, she reminded me of the baby monitor. She remembered the nights that I had forgotten to turn it off. She would be awakened to my heartbroken howls. She cried as I cycled through raging anger, punching the pillows or screaming into them. It took all her strength not to rush across the house to comfort me, but she knew that I was grieving. After some weeks, some months – she couldn't remember – my repetition of 'I can't live like this' ceased. Somehow, she took it to mean that I wasn't going to live with this depression, rather than disability. I knew you'd come back to us after you had grieved enough, she said.

Momo remembers that first Christmas visit as a moment when she could breathe again. That I was still in this world, her world. She was going to be okay because I would be okay. The universe had handed her a gilded excuse to take a drink. Her only son almost died and was now disabled.

She says, Nobody would have blamed me if I drank, but I knew it wasn't going to do you any good. It wasn't going to do me any good either.

We are talking on the phone, and I ask her about it. She is in her backyard to smoke and let her new puppy out. Her shouts – Get out of there. That's a no, little shithead – occasionally interrupt our conversation.

A few months before my accident she started a women-only AA group called the ROSE group: Recovering Our Self-Esteem. Every Tuesday they met in a room at the back of a Methodist church. She started the group to help others, but it was the group that kept her sober.

Before I can ask another question Momo goes off on a tangent. She says she sometimes goes down the booze aisle to see all the new alcohol flavours. She marvels at hard root beer and wonders what hard seltzer tastes like. Newly sober, she replaced the habit of spending nights working through cases of beer by drinking flavoured seltzer water. That now they are adding cheap grain alcohol to it amuses her. When she worked downtown, she deliberately passed by the Gator Club, a notorious local boozer, to take a nostalgic noseful of the stale-beer-and-cigarettes smell. But she can't stand to be around drunks. We agree on that. It comes from an anxiety from long ago that we don't have to name.

The first time I met the women from the ROSE group was at a Perkins, a chain restaurant known for its pies. In her first sober years, afraid of going home and being alone, Momo went to Perkins after her AA meetings. Perkins saved my life, she said, which is a way better slogan than their 'Breakfast is just the beginning'.

Momo made introductions as the women took their seats at the table. Susan, her sponsor, was a brassy my-way-or-the-highway New Yorker. There was Danielle, her best friend, who started the Rose group with her, a sponsee Linda, who would later return to drinking and never come back, the thought of which always makes Momo sad, and a flower-seller and wise woman named Fudgie.

Finally, Marilyn, in her seventies, arrived without a tooth in her head, dressed somewhere between bag lady and showgirl. She came from Manhattan gentry and before she got sober, was a street prostitute. In her words: from Park Lane to park bench. She was known for hitting on younger men at AA meetings with promises that she 'knew things most girls don't' while smacking her toothless gums.

Marilyn, do you remember Jarred? And this is his angel, Sarah.

Angel? Who's this angel? I only ever heard you call her the 'whore who raped your son'.

Momo! Sarah said.

I didn't say that, Momo said as her cheeks went red.

Yes, you did, I said.

After going back to school and getting my degree in Austin, Texas, Sarah and I moved to the UK. I remember the first time I saw Trafalgar Square. High above us mortals stood the famous amputee and boating enthusiast Lord Nelson with an empty coat sleeve pinned neatly to his chest and his sightless granite eye. The Marc Quinn sculpture *Alison Lapper Pregnant* was behind him upon the altar of the fourth plinth. As I was crossing the street and thinking how lucky I was to have chosen a country where the disabled were worshipped as gods, a white van with a large dog in the driver's seat almost hit me without slowing. A shout came from an angry bald man in what I thought was the passenger side of the car, Watch it, you wheelie bastard.

The exact moment I knew I wanted to be a dad was when my sister-in-law's daughter hugged me. Those full-bodied hugs that babies do. Where you feel the transcendent geometry of them. How they feel so heavy and light at the same time, insubstantial from having barely arrived on Earth. They carry no weight of experience, good or bad. Their feet barely touch here. And yet, who they are is there compressed into those small bodies and enormous heads, so fragile and robust, containing the density of their entire life's mass to be consumed.

On one of our visits back to Florida, we stayed with my sister-in-law. My niece and I were on the couch together, and I was looking through a magazine and making up stories about the people in the pictures. She, being a toddler and illiterate, was none the wiser. I turned the page to find a photo of Nosferatu in a Marilyn Monroe wig. It was a feature article about Joan Rivers, a monster of a different sort. *Once upon a time, there was a beautiful, talented girl from the Catskills who one night was bit by an evil count and TV producer, dooming her to a living-dead existence, hiding under red carpets to spread a pestilence of self-hatred.*

This little girl was enraptured by my improvised tale

of terror using only the article's photos of Rivers's leaf-blowered face and hollow eyes. I was feeling pretty good about my performance as an uncle until the next day at breakfast when my sister-in-law told me that her daughter had a terrible, sleepless night. It didn't make any sense, she said. She was shouting about Joan Rivers being under her bed, at least that's what I think she was saying.

I agreed that it didn't make any sense at all.

Later, I explained to my niece that Joan Rivers, being a creature of darkness, cannot stand the sun. Since we were in sunny Florida, there was little risk that she would be flapping her wig to scrape her varnished claws at our windows. However, there were precautions we could take, such as cloves of garlic and a general sense of body positivity. The lich of QVC haunted my niece's bedtime thoughts less and less, though my sister-in-law was concerned about the garlic-bulb dolls that her daughter had secreted around the room as a ward against the taut-faced one.

Later that week we drove past the events centre advertising Joan Rivers' upcoming show with a six-metre digital display of her undead visage. Luckily my niece was in her car seat playing with the Mr Garlic Head I made her – a ballpoint face drawn on the bulb's paper. I had to explain to my sister-in-law what I had done so she avoided driving past the events centre for a few days. I don't remember her being upset but she wisely suggested I stick with age-appropriate children's books from now on.

Our GP was unconcerned; he said to keep trying. We felt no urgency. We have time. Still, we didn't tell anyone we were trying for children from an unspoken shame, as if we were failing at a basic qualification of humanity. Each month a thin grey rime covered everything in our lives when it was clear Sarah wasn't pregnant. At first, it was a dusting, a taste of bitter salts. Certainly, we didn't discuss it. We brushed it off the breakfast table; we shook it from the sheets of our bed; we wiped it from our mouths. Month after month, the accretion thickened in the corners where we were less attentive.

After two years of 'keep trying' a statistical milestone was reached, and a box was ticked. We had just started the process of understanding the source of the infertility issues when Sarah was diagnosed with cervical cancer. She crossed the hospital's central atrium from the fertility clinic to the cancer ward. It was aggressive but treatable. There was a survival rate of over 90 per cent. How surprisingly life went on normally with a one in ten chance of her death.

When I talk to Sarah about this time, she says, I don't remember it like that. I didn't think of it as having cancer or one in ten. It was a procedure I had to have done. You were so worried though. Decades together and I still haven't learned this wisdom of hers. She is the rock, and I am the thrashing sea.

We went to work, filed our taxes, waited for tables at restaurants, scrolled on our phones – all while she went through the NHS cursus honorum of appointments: blood tests, a colposcopy, consultations and finally the surgery. The surgeons felt confident that they cut out all the cancerous cells, but she would have years of follow-ups to be sure. She took a week off to recover. She was sore, but she could move around and take care of herself. I was meant to go to the Frankfurt Book Fair for work. Sarah assured me that she would be fine. I pre-made her some meals for the week and submitted to the indignities that air travel doles out to wheelchair users like tiny bags of pretzels.

When I have been sitting in my wheelchair too long, a dull ache creeps into my right ankle. On my second day in Frankfurt, neuropathic pain spread to other spots below my waist until it was like a fireworks display. Explosions of electric fire spread across my legs and groin. I knew that if I laid down it would subside. While everyone was distracted by Paulo Coelho seeing how many cookies he could fit in his mouth, I went back to my hotel. Instead, it got worse, and my heart beat out irregular triplets. Washes of cold sweat climbed up my body as I tried to take deep breaths. I picked up the phone to call the front desk to call the ambulance. I put it down. I put on the TV. I messaged Sarah to say good night and I'd talk to her in the morning.

The paradiddles in my chest grew more frequent. My fear grew. I turned off the TV. TV on. TV off. Pick up a book. I couldn't focus. TV, no TV. Book, no book. My fingers started to tingle. Is that just the anxiety or a symptom? Deep breath. Deep. Breath. A pressure built against my ribs as if a child had climbed onto my chest. He sat there, looking down to see how I would react. Something bad was happening.

I rang the front desk, Could you call an ambulance? I'm not feeling well, something with my heart. The paramedics in the ambulance and the staff at the hospital were patient with my miming the symptoms as they wheeled me to get an ultrasound and wired me for an ECG. Eventually, I met a cardiologist who was excited to use his English and talk about his recent holiday to Cornwall. He explained the arrhythmia came from one side of my heart, a few branches of nerve that get out of time. That was a good thing. If it was the other side, it was life-threatening.

Are you dealing with any stress right now? he asked. When I mentioned Sarah's recent surgery, I realised I had been playing at being tough and brave and not scared of a one-in-ten chance of my world collapsing. I recalled almost nothing of the past months. I had ignored my fear and anxiety to minister in whatever tiny way until she was okay. Now that she was, those emotions bubbled forth and made me think I was having a heart attack. It made sense now. The doctor talked about his previous bicycle trips around Scotland. I wasn't listening. I was thinking about Sarah. I think about Sarah now. That I can barely recall those months of her being ill feels like a denial of what she experienced. She assures me that I was a good husband. I was there and supportive during the whole ordeal.

A nurse put me into a room where from the window I saw the church that the hospital was named for. The other bed was empty. On the wall beside me was a crucifix. Below it was a bright red bin bag for contaminated waste and on either side were two poles for intravenous drips, an altar of a kind.

My heart was still occasionally stumbling through its repertoire but picked up the four-four beat more readily. Despite the light levels and constant noise, I find hospitals comfortable. The beds are soft. It is a place of care. Here people help, but I had trouble falling asleep.

There was a presence that occupied the visitor's chair.

It was a boy, but there was a translucence to him. His skin was thin and the net of capillaries beneath tinged him red. His puffy eyelids seemed closed, but I caught a glimpse of the black pupils moving over me and the room.

When I was eleven or twelve, we had moved to a barrier island off the coast of Florida. A splinter of sand called Siesta Key that the Gulf of Mexico tides constantly worried at. Dad was a vanishing presence in this house, number 99, so that when Mom and he split up, I didn't notice the difference. At the time, I had the late eighties mullet à la Karate Kid (as played by nice guy from Long Island, Ralph Macchio, famed for his ability to play a nice guy from Long Island). The presence in that German hospital room, called there by anxiety or adverse side effects of medication, had that haircut.

He was dressed like me at that age, in shorts, and a T-shirt with a logo that I couldn't quite make out. No shoes, though. Within the translucent rich red of his feet floated the shadows of toe bones like a morse code. Like me at that age, he had a silver hoop earring. This presence that was me-not-me when I was younger sat there motionless. We looked at each other. His voice was thin and unsure, but it was a boy's voice.

Your problem is that you have no problems, he said.

That sounds like something I would say to my kids.

You will.

Once again, we stopped trying for a child until Sarah's regular check-ups made sure she was cancer-free. The options for cancer treatment during pregnancy were too grim to risk. By the time Sarah got the all-clear, we were eligible for a round of IVF. The doctor explained what it entailed. IVF is a brutality of needles and false hope. We still didn't tell anyone. On one of our weekly video calls with Momo, she made her usual joke about dying before we have kids, and I retorted that I'd love to give her a grandchild, but Sarah likes it in the pooper. Momo shouted at me. Sarah told me to cut it out.

About a year or so after my accident, the hardware on my spine had developed osteomyelitis, an infection that ate at my bones. After the surgery I was prescribed a course of industrial-strength antibiotics and appointments to a wound clinic where we were surrounded by late-stage diabetics whose big toes had rotted off. The black hole at the end of a leg reminded me of the exploding cigars in a Bugs Bunny cartoon, a brash of bone instead of ash clinging to the swollen foot. At the clinic, they showed us how to clean my wounds so that Sarah could do it at home. And she did. Both of us awed at the disgusting miracle of the human body as she drew out the bloody purulent length of gauze as if it was a magician's scarf. We were proud of her steadfastness when she tucked a fresh sterile gauze into the horror show teddy bear of me. And yet, she cannot get her blood drawn without passing out. She has a phobia of needles, so I gave her the daily IVF shots. It was horrible every time but easier to endure after the first few. And yet, what beautiful pearls those moments have made. A test of what we would do for each other and do it unflinchingly. With time it is only the opalescence that remains. I can see in my memories my hesitation to stick her with the needle. Her averting her eyes. The pinch of skin between my fingers, the dribble of medicine, the redness, the agitation of her flesh, the soreness after I pushed the plunger. I was able to care for Sarah as she has cared for me. It has mostly been her at the bedside when the general anaesthetic wore off. Paraplegia isn't just great parking and inspiring unimaginative strangers. Osteomyelitis is just one of the possible Latinate-based sufferings on offer. Gallstones and cholecystectomy, that's when a doctor steals your gall bladder, which everyone knows is where the animus soul of a human resides. I am at my most amusing, Sarah has told me, on Dilaudid.

At the end of the month of daily injections, they collected her eggs. I was beside her when she woke up. She didn't know where she was. I soothed her fear, unused to the reversal of roles. Mostly, I knew she wouldn't have liked that she was scared and vulnerable, and more so being seen as scared and vulnerable.

My part in all of it was limited to a small room with two chairs and a little door set in the wall where I was to deposit a specimen jar, shut the little door and knock on it. I amused myself with the thought of banging on the walls, howling and then after a moment of silence, opening the technician's side and directly handing off the specimen with a cheery 'here you go' and sustained eye contact. I planned to tell Sarah that was what I had done, and she would smile and roll her eyes. The distinctly not-fun of producing the sample ruined that idea. The A4 document box between the two chairs held a couple of well-perused magazines with ridiculous names like *Fiesta* and *Knave*. I opened a magazine to the reader submissions section. Instead of titillation, I found a photo showing the corner of a mattress exposed and the crumple of sheets behind a pale slab of skin at the centre. The top of a nightstand was hidden under fast food containers, bottles of Lucozade, wadded tissues and other detritus. The naked young woman beneath a dishevelled blonde topknot looked uncertain and uncomfortable. I put the magazine back and looked around the small room. I felt disgusted by my flippancy.

After the embryo transfer, a fertility specialist and statistical probability told us a baby was not going to be. Neither of us was in a rush to repeat the month-long trial knowing it would be just as bad and that the chances of success were even more minuscule. Those years and years when we were trying unsuccessfully to have a baby by both natural and medically induced means, we were alone and ashamed. Friends and acquaintances had dashed their relationship against the obsession to have a baby, traumatising themselves at great expense to deny what fate had insisted. In my marriage vow, I talked about adventures built for two. We would stick with that plan and not sacrifice what we had for what might have been. I thought I had made my peace with that.

As Sarah and I were crossing a street, a black cab pulled
to the red a little too fast and stopped a little too hard.
I snapped. I lost control. Invectives flew from my lips.
I saw the driver's face through the glass show surprise,
then amusement, then laughter. I was the angry cripple
of people's expectations. I saw myself. The ridiculousness
of my overreaction. The way Sarah was embarrassed and
afraid.

Later that night, I couldn't sleep so I went into the
living room so as not to disturb Sarah. The presence had
returned. He was on our couch watching a muted TV
with his huge black eyes barely visible from beneath his
puffy lids.

You guys aren't going to have kids? he asked, without
looking away from the silent car insurance commercial. I
watched the crowd mouthing the words to the song about
fifteen per cent savings, dancing around parked cars in a
cul-de-sac.

It looks like, I said. I moved to the couch, locked my
brakes and transferred over to sit beside him.

Are you sad?

Yes.

You had me.

Yes.

Then you got rid of me.

I know.

Do you think this is punishment?

Sometimes. And sometimes I think, fair enough. I'm sorry. Do you want to hear the reasons?

I know why.

Okay, I said. Are you Bishop?

Could've been. It's not punishment though. That's not how this works. No one deserves the bad things that happen, but you don't deserve the good either.

He was animated when he said this. It seemed an important truth that he understood but it put him off balance. His oversized head flopped back into the corner, and he slid forward. He flailed as he tried to right himself.

Let me help, I said and shifted closer to him. He was warm to the touch. And soft, and delicate, and unnerving. Sorry, I said, as I awkwardly helped right him.

You said that. Do you want to talk about why I'm here?

Not sure what I have to say.

You are now experiencing the brittle fixedness of actuality. Be glad that it's taken nearly forty years for its weight to be felt. You've been here before, but you were too busy dying under a truck to pay attention.

We sat and watched a muted *Seinfeld* episode. He flinched at the jerky motions of Kramer.

I wasn't ready to be a dad, I said. I wouldn't have handled it well. We were too young.

It's okay, you know.

I would have failed you.

You would have missed out on a lot of things too.

I agreed. He was right. It's hard to argue with a metre-tall foetus. We stayed silent. I felt the building pressure to talk, but he spoke first.

It could have been as you said. It could have been a disaster. It is possible that you would have ended up back in Florida . . . But that's not why.

No. But yes too.

He nodded and played with the marvel of his hair.

It's dark like yours. Blue-black.

I know, right? The last time I imagined you, you hinted that I would have kids.

He stared at me. He said, I said that your problem is that you have no problems.

A bit harsh considering I am a paraplegic. I've got the parking decal and everything.

Harsh but fair. You have inconveniences, microaggressions from the universe. A dimple of discomfort compared to the oceanic trenches suffered by others. Your cancers will be survived in relative comfort and in air-conditioned hospitals. Have the decency to recognise that.

You've got an answer for everything.

I am related to you.

What do you want me to say? How many times does a fertilised egg come to nothing? You had a few extra weeks of cell division but ultimately an insignificance. You weren't real. There was no quickening. I won't have that life with you either. Good or bad but that's how it is. Why are you haunting me?

Is that what I'm doing?
What would you call it?

I remember how violently ill Sarah was. That's how we knew. After a doctor's appointment, a pill and a few painful hours, it was over. I felt sadness. Not at the abortion but that Sarah wasn't well. Once it was over, we never really thought about it again until we were trying to get pregnant, and she had to write down her previous pregnancies.

Zed and Maude

I emailed Grandpa to congratulate him about his promotion to *great*-grandpa, and his response was to email a genealogy. Each generation of McGinnis was numbered and followed by 'firstborn male child'. After the line '7. (firstborn male child) Jarred Patrick McGinnis', he wrote '8. (firstborn male child) London McGinnis'.

Of course, the firstborn to the seventh-generation firstborn son of a firstborn son would be male. At the time, the sex was unknown, but Grandpa assumed. We all assumed, just as it had been assumed that my mom's womb held a green-eyed, black-haired son. However, it was also assumed that my name would be William O'Bannon McGinnis, the fourth. It wasn't a matter for discussion. With Bill, William, and Will taken, I would have ended up being a Willy. No child deserves that, and Momo chose her moments for rebellion wisely as each battle was costly. By naming me Jarred, I think she was trying to claim some of her son for herself. The middle name of Patrick was chosen as a peace offering to the more-Oirish-than-the-Irish American McGinnises.

Sarah, twenty weeks pregnant, was led to the table. The ultrasound machine beside her emanated benevolence. A ceremony began. The lights dimmed; the machine switched on. A libation of warmed gel applied to her stomach. Then the miracle. From pixelated swirls, an arm emerged, a head, a face! From the machine's speakers, tinny static solidified, becoming a heartbeat. The beat sounded fast, too fast, but the technician, practised in parent-to-be worries, said that it was normal for a foetus.

Sorry, she said, foetuses. It's twins . . . Fraternal. Do you want to know the sexes?

A swirl of static, a blur of pixels, and the magic eight ball of ultrasound said: two females.

We looked at each other, stunned. Scared but excited. My immediate impulse was to ask about risks, complications and potential outcomes. I craved the comfort of statistical likelihoods for Sarah and our babies.

I said, We're going to need a bigger car.

A bigger flat, Sarah replied.

These beings who were supposed to be an impossibility now were urgently announcing their existences with a double-time thdump from the ultrasound's speakers. Sarah, who had felt these hidden presences, whose body was changing daily, wept too.

We thrilled at telling the family that it was a girl and, after a dramatic pause, saying she had a sister.

I expected a snipe about the gender from grandpa. Those responses did come from other family but never from him. He sent an amended genealogy with the genders removed and changing the last line to London McGinnis

#1 and London McGinnis #2. When I responded that I was excited to introduce him to his first great-grandchildren, he replied, 'ME TOOOO!!!' Case, number of 'o's and punctuation were so uncharacteristic that I thought it was my aunt emailing.

Shortly after the appointment with the endocrinologist declining further rounds of IVF, we had gone to Greece to attend the baptism of our friends' twins. The service was in an ancient church made to accommodate fifty. Two hundred were in attendance. Aunties were everywhere, moving chairs, sneaking behind the priest onto the altar to take better photos. One knocked the censer hanging on the wall. People went in and out for smoke breaks. The priest, like a dour version of Santa dressed like a wizard, performed the ceremony in a foul temper. More aunties were shouting and pointing out the spots the priest missed when rubbing the babies in olive oil in their belief that the child would always smell bad if a spot remained unanointed.

A month after we returned, Sarah came into the bedroom saying she had news. I got excited because I assumed the orange kitten who had been coming to our back garden had returned.

No, she said and handed me the pregnancy strip.

What about the cat? I asked, not noticing the second blue line.

There's no cat, Jarred. I'm pregnant.

When we told our Greek friends, they were unsurprised.

Of course, they said. You spent a week on a Greek beach eating yoghurt, honey and walnuts with our little ones.

I have always admired Sarah, but during her pregnancy, I could brag to strangers, she was making humans, inside her, right now. When we first dated, I loved to go to parties, stand across the room and watch her be Sarah. I used to spread rumours about her at the party so that at some point inevitably someone asked her about her time as a fireman in Dresden or her experiences as a hermaphrodite. I had told them that she had a cute, the cutest, little penis, like a shrew's nose. It was my way of flirting. She has said, Flowers are nice too, you know.

Sarah and I celebrated each new development. We followed the apps that describe the size of the foetus, from sesame seeds to melons. When the quickening happened, we spooned so I could feel the kicks and punches.

She reminds me that I also referred to her pregnancy as when she was hogging the babies, and that, at one of the NHS-arranged antenatal classes, I thought it was funny to ask, If my baby is born ugly, do I still have to feed it?

Momo came to London for the births and we got a few days with her to explore a London dressed handsomely in its winter greys. We went to the hospital on Thursday afternoon and Sarah was given a pessary to induce birth. By Friday morning, contractions had started. We strolled the hospital halls. She had to pause to ride out the contractions, just like in the movies. By the evening, though, labour wasn't progressing, and the doctors were getting nervous. Saturday morning, they broke her waters with a crochet hook where God and textile art never intended. Still nothing, and Sarah felt disappointed as if she was to blame. Her discomfort continued to grow, and she asked for her foam pillow from home. Our flat was only a fifteen-minute walk, ten by wheelchair, from the hospital. I left her the book I had brought.

Back at the flat, Momo had all she needed: snacks, books, and heat. She had recreated the temperature and humidity of her native Florida, sitting on the couch reading with the space heater inches from her legs. I told her I had no news, but Sarah was fine. Uncomfortable but fine. If breaking her waters didn't work, they were recommending an IV induction and an epidural. Sarah had hoped to avoid both but in the words of Mike Tyson's father, the well-known OB/GYN, 'Everyone has a plan until they have a human's skull punching through their cervix.'

It was dark by the time I returned and the road that connected the hospital was frequented by prostitutes. It was a sad road to traverse. The younger ones were bold and drug addled. The older women with eyes of trapped animals were more furtive. Inevitably they looked to me, a man, for an invitation. I always felt embarrassed, passing them with averted eyes. A woman asked me if I had a date for tonight. I stopped. We looked at each other. She repeated her question. She looked at my lap where Sarah's requested pillow sat. The absurdity of a john bringing his own pillow momentarily lightened the moment.

This is for my wife, I said. My daughters are about to

be born. I pointed out the rooftop of the hospital above council estate.

Be lucky, she said.

Thank you, I said.

When I arrived, the midwife gave me a hard time about the book I left, which I thought was a bit odd – surely reading is good for the mother-to-be. Sarah told me that the opening scene was a particularly gruesome and tragic labour. We took a moment to reflect on the goofball our children would be saddled with as a father.

By the middle of the night, the IV had begun its work. Sarah kept wanting to raise herself from the bed as the contractions overtook her, but the midwife kept pushing her down, saying it was dangerous because of the epidural. I intuited that the time for goofing off with the gas and air was over. I sat beside her, touching her, not touching her, at her caprice. While she was resting before the next wave, I thought it would be a good idea to turn off my phone. She spoke through gritted teeth, Are you on your phone? I explained but she didn't listen. Weeks later I mentioned how mean she was when she was in labour and she looked at me directly and clearly said, I don't care.

At one point during the labour, she slumped over after a contraction. The midwife assured me that she was asleep, that this happens. The body knew what she needed, and she was okay.

The first daughter, Zora, arrived early Sunday morning with a rattling howl at the pokes and prods. Given the potential problems of a twin birth, the doctors were pleased with progress, but soon Maude was showing signs of distress. An emergency Caesarean was organised. When we tell the girls the story of their birth, we tell Maude, the second born, that her ears got stuck. They put up a blue sterile curtain to obscure the view of Sarah's belly sliced open from ilium to ilium. I tried not to look at the bloodied instruments the curtain failed to hide. It's not a gentle procedure. We are meat, and surgery is butcher's work in nitrate gloves. After the days of labour and whatever sauce they were topping up her IV with, Sarah passed out. Her inert body rocked as they pulled our daughter from her. The medical team worked quietly and efficiently and, in that bright silence of the operating theatre, I heard my Maude's first tentative complaint, not quite removed from the womb, vagitus, a strange phenomenon worthy of Latin like the aurora borealis. It was still a few moments before they lifted her above the curtain. They held her under her arms. She was more bluish-purple than her sister. Her arms and fingers were spread wide, but it was her eyes that startled me. They looked about her as if surprised to find herself here amongst us. She wasn't upset or crying, just surprised. It wasn't until they put her under the heat lamps that she howled full of life. Those first cries from them both brought the sharp and sudden understanding there were species of love I had not known until that moment. As Sarah slept, they handed me two tightly swaddled bundles. A man in a wheelchair, forever with a lap, is better for holding newborn twins than the average father. Sarah woke up in the recovery room with her babies and me beside her. It was much darker and quieter there. The midwife put the girls in her arms. Sarah noticed a birth-mark on one twin's left eye and a corresponding mark above her sister's right eye. Sister freckles, she noted with pleasure.

What're are you thinking with the names? I asked.

This is Zee Zee, she said and gave one of the bundles a jiggle. I had dreamed of a daughter named Zora Zola McGinnis, named for my two favourite authors. Zee Zee for short, Zed now that we've moved to France and found out Zee Zee means penis.

Then this must be Maude, I said to the second born, who had her colour by then. Sarah picked the name from the film *Harold and Maude*. She was a little too tiny, but both were healthy. My problem is that I have no problems. That one was born obligingly and the other had to be dragged out is now part of their mythology. We recount what tiny babies they were and that the only way to tell the difference was that Zed's head looked like a peanut and Maude had a pig's tail. Thank God for that tail, we joke, and have shown the girls the dried husk of umbil-ical cord as proof. Zed calls herself the real daughter and her sister a zipper baby.

Sarah was in hospital with the girls for about a week before they could all go home.

What outfit did you bring? Sarah asked, sore but mobile.

The kitty zombie ones. I held up the little outfits with smiling kitties and their exposed brains.

Those are pink tiaras, not brains.

*

That new love I felt hearing Maude's little squeak of a cry still in the womb and Zed's full-throated yowl when she announced her arrival was not new at all. For years, I had mistaken my love for Sarah as the romantic love that is sold to men from boyhood. I felt aggrieved that I had never fathomed the true depth of adoration for my wife until I held our newborn daughters. I immediately felt the need to apologise to Sarah, but it was too abstract an emotion at too fraught a moment. It was time to be here in this Now with these tiny humans and the bond connecting us, thrumming in the winds of the universe.

Our families bought us Finnish baby boxes decorated with Moomins that arrived filled with everything you would need for the first few months of a new baby: clothing including teeny-weeny socks for their teeny-weeny little feet, blankets, various postpartum toiletries for mom, baby-care stuff for baby and, optimistically, condoms. The boxes had padding at the bottom and the bed linens they came with turned the box into baby's first crib. We set them on Sarah's side of the bed so she could more easily feed the twins. We'd go to bed and in the dark stillness of night fall asleep to the sound of newborn fingernails scrabbling against the boxes as if we had rodents in the walls. Most of the time, though, the babies slept tucked against Sarah where they could feed with a minimal amount of motion and disturbance to her sleep. The brimming cup of anxiety so eagerly handed to new parents was ignored. This felt right, and that you would crush your baby while sleeping was an absurdity. Every bit of our attention conscious or otherwise was tuned to their slightest peep of discomfort. I still flinch when I hear a baby cry. Their real cry, not that Mickey Mouse fake nonsense they try to see if you'll jump for them. Babies are sneaky like that.

To celebrate the children who were not meant to be, Sarah took the full year of maternity. To make the money last, we left London and lived elsewhere and more cheaply. When we came back, the girls had been to twenty countries. This will be another story in their mythology.

It was inarguable that we would visit my grandfather. Before that, we spent some time just us four, happily collapsing our world to Sarah and me and these new humans who had been our first and foremost wish for so long.

On that first day in Mexico, the babies were tucked against Sarah's chest in a wrap, completely incurious about the setting sun drawing closer to the grey-blue endlessness of the Pacific. On the rocks nearby, brown pelicans struck poses regal and absurd. Around us was the marvel of purple shadows flanking the horizon that could have been mountains or clouds.

I was enjoying the familiar humidity and heat from my childhood in the subtropics, after the adult decades beneath the low-hung chill of London. Shirtless men armed with cast nets battled over a plunder of fish with the frigatebirds, an animal made for war with its long-bladed wings. What do you call these fish? I asked a whip of a boy, wearing only Spider-Man underwear. He threw the dagger-shaped fish into a bucket.

Cariños, he said. I looked up the word. It means sweetheart.

We arrived in May, the off-season. The Old Town of Puerto Vallarta is a grid of colonial buildings full of gay bars to entertain older and wealthier American tourists who come for the mild winters here. The tourism board has been trying to rebrand the area as

Zona Romantica. There's a bar called 'Wet Dreams' with a sign that says, 'No Women'. Inside, you can order a beer and watch a handsome young man suds his body in a glass shower, which is romance of a kind. People live in the Zona as well. The shaded stairwells between buildings are full of families poking at their phones as they hide from the day's heat. Old Town is separated from the America-in-miniature walled resorts to the north by the trickle of the Río Cuale. Closer to the airport, the pretence of Mexico is dropped completely, and it is just strip malls bookended by McDonald's and TGI Fridays.

The Spanish of Mexico is great for baby talk. My cheeks bulged with the chubby-ankled syllables and round, rolling Rs that people handed me on our walks. It is a perfect language to give my daughters more nicknames than ancient gods: cariño, abejita, bonita, chamaquita, preciosa, tierna. Everyone we met was baby crazy. Gangs of tattooed teenage boys cooed as much as the frequent encirclements of grandmas. We had to get used to strangers rubbing our babies' heads and brushing their cheeks uninvited. Though fraternal twins, they looked exactly alike. Exceptionally bald heads, perfectly round. They resembled 1:12-scale models of Soviet politburo members. I had compounded the problem by thinking it was funny to dress them in baby-sized guayabera shirts that matched my own. Our walks along the promenade were interrupted every few feet to let anyone from the police to fishermen make silly faces and invoke one of their thousand nicknames. We loved it. A whole nation sharing the marvel of these humans. In a crowded taqueria, the owner passed the girls around the regulars and the kitchen staff. Look at these chuletas, he crowed. Look at these little porkchops. Of all the names we brought back with us, years later, they are still my chuletas.

Of all the clichés about parenting, no one talks about how easy time travel becomes. There is a shift in self, you no longer fully exist in the present. You draw the past to you so it cannot attack your newborn. Simultaneously, a baby creates futures impossible before their arrival.

The first time I felt the sickening flip through time was the day we burned Zed. We were looking for a post office and got turned around in the grid of sidewalks three feet above the streets clotted with CENTRO buses and yellow cabs that catcalled 'taxi' at us. The cost of our mistake was stripes of sunburn on our daughter's arms and legs where she poked out from Sarah's wrap. Zed was the squirmiest of the two. There was always a leg working its way out of the wrap or a hand stretching out in search of her sister's cheek. When Maude was in the wrap, she instantly fell asleep, lullabied by her mother's heartbeat.

We stopped to rest under a beach palapa so Sarah could go look for water and sunburn cream while Zed and I made the most of an ocean breeze. Zed was naked except for a cool wet cloth on her head. Though she was more fussy than usual, she didn't, couldn't, blame me. I asked for forgiveness anyway, dabbing at her sunburn with an aloe that I had harvested from a hotel's landscaping.

I settled her down on my bare chest. She was still baby-tiny but, at almost double her birth weight, substantial in a new way. That moment with our skin touching and the compact weight of her, balled up as if still in utero, whipped us forward nine months. Zed and Maude are one. We are back in London and our flat. Maternity leave has ended, and Sarah is back at work. The babies are still stubbornly bald. Zed is walking by holding on to my wheelchair and working her way around me, giggling with excitement at her new ability. She drops back down and crawls away. She aims straight for an electric plug, which she puts in her mouth. I yell at her, a forceful 'no' more from fear than anger. I scoop her up and feel the heart racing within the fragile shell of ribs as she draws breath to work herself into an ugly pantomime cry. As a dad, I thought I had rejected that exhausting need for obedience and the ready-made anger I knew. But this little girl will be afraid of me. I will be frightening just as my father was frightening to me and his father to him.

Are you okay? Sarah said to me. Zed was a three-month-old again, asleep and tucked against me, my hand rubbing her back. I was back on the beach in Mexico. Sarah had returned with a bottle of child-safe sun cream in her hand and Maude asleep in her wrap. I said I was fine but in me was the knowledge that I would be the one to seed fear into my daughter's heart.

My soon-to-be-parents are on their way to New Mexico. My father has finished basic training and is reporting for his first duty station in the Air Force. If that's right, I would be born a year or so later.

Even now as an elderly woman, there's something of the little girl about my mom. It is a part of her character that is endearing, frustrating and essential. My childhood is filled with memories of her in the ice-cream shop pointing with excitement at all the flavours before inevitably choosing her favourite, Rocky Road. Momo often tells me she was a fat child. That she stole food from her smaller, younger sister. She told me that in third grade at show-and-tell she would hold up pictures of desserts torn from magazines and repeat, Yum yum yum, until the teacher thanked her and asked her to sit down.

As they passed strip mall after strip mall with their empty oceans of parking lots, Momo spotted a Baskin-Robbins. With a bounce, she asked if they could stop and get an ice cream.

Without turning his head from the red light, my dad

says, You know, I wanted an ice cream and I was going to stop, but you had to go and ask for it. So now I'm not going to stop and none of us get an ice cream.

When the light turns green, he drives without another word. The happiness melts from my mom as she sinks into her seat.

I was unprepared for the emotional rawness that came with the birth of my daughters. It was there all the time. I wept easily and often. Sometimes for the pure joy of witnessing their existence, because a reproductive endocrinologist and a failed round of IVF had said they were a statistical unlikelihood. Sometimes I cry from old grievances thought forgotten.

Sarah had made her family's sweet-and-sour pork recipe. Without warning, sitting at the dinner table, chattering away as we often do, I wept because both of my daughters were smiling at me.

The bond between daughters and mother was instant, a chemical reaction catalysed by whatever secrets passed in utero. After the days of labour and the emergency Caesarean had left Sarah hollowed, she slept while the doctors sutured and cauterised the damage. As they cleaned and checked my second born, I held Zed. She tried to focus on my face, but she couldn't. Her eyes tracked up, fell, and up again. An hour later, in recovery, when she saw her mother, her eyes locked onto my wife's and that thrumming, unbreakable connection was made. All other relationships would be secondary; my role in those first months was auxiliary, but I relished it. The changer of nappies, the fixer of tea and toast, the consolation for the babies when Mom needed five minutes, just five minutes, to shower. Now a few months later, with care and attention, they had begun to understand me as a constancy in their lives.

That moment on that beach in Mexico where I saw that my girls would fear me came back to me as we sat at the table. I wept, because I was loved by these two new humans. I wept, because my father beat me and because his father beat him and because his father . . .

Was it inevitable that this all-consuming desire to protect your children, unarmed and ill-prepared for the world's ugliness, dissipates and it is you, their father, who introduces them to violence? It's even more frightening that only few years later, I understood how easily it could happen. A flash of anger taken too far and then a moment that can't be taken back, then another, and so on, until you wrap your actions in excuses or denials. All those memories of your child's seemingly miraculous firsts of crawling, eating, laughing, walking, lose their power. In the first months, when one of the babies cried, it sent a shiv of anxiety through me until I bought a pair of ground-crew earmuffs to be able to minister to them. The smell of their hair, the feel of their skin against my cheek, the moments where they tuck the immensity of their being into the small space made by the cradle of my arms, 'Papa's nook', can suddenly mean nothing. That scared me more than anything.

The family tradition of abuse and alcoholism stopped

with me. None of those men before me said, It stopped with me. What is worse is that each one of them, every generation, claimed that it would stop with them. Surely, they believed that no matter what, they would not subject their son to what their father had done to them. Every generation saw themselves lift their ten-year-old son off the ground. Seven heavy knuckled hands holding seven boys by their throats. Each man holding a whiskey in their other hand. The ice clacking against glasses for over a century against the useless struggle of those helpless boys, but never once was a drop spilled.

My father never beat me in the morning, as his father beat him, just in case I might do something bad that he wouldn't find out about. He never beat me in front of a girl I brought home when I was sixteen. He never pulled me out of bed while I was sleeping and dropped me on my head. My father was a damaged boy who became a damaged man and a damaged father. Perversely, it was my appreciation of what my father suffered that has always made it hard to write him off completely. I go back and forth about whether my father was a bad man. I remember fond moments with my dad as the actions of a kind and funny man. Other times, they appear as the calculated moves of an egotist who knew he would need our forgiveness eventually.

At thirteen I was incarcerated and invited him to one of my psychiatric appointments. His physical abuse of me and my mom, and his erratic, sometimes cruel behaviour had more than a measure of responsibility for why I was locked up. After polite introductions and manly handshakes between him and the psychiatrist, we sat in the small, cluttered office. I told him that it would be better if I never saw him again. His neutral facial expression, the measured agreements to my demands, and my projection of the indignity he felt at having this credentialled stranger privy to our family shame, added to my fears. I didn't understand Dad's blank responses. It was uncharted territory. Here be dragons.

After numerous incidents when his relapses have affected my life and my loved ones, I have asked myself, am I to blame? Do I remind him of that day? Sometimes, I take it more personally. Is it because I'm disabled? His only son is a cripple. If there's a reason for a drink, that's one.

It is the unpredictability of my father that haunts me more than the blue-sky lightning strikes of violence. He hung me by one foot over bridges as a joke on multiple occasions. I remember my dad inviting me to look over the edge of Stone Mountain, a 250-metre-high bulge of granite rising out of the forest near Atlanta, Georgia. The rock is also the world's largest commemoration of traitors to the United States. I fell to the ground, gripping the granite hysterical with fear, not trusting him. It is up to me that my daughters never experience the confusing and frightening world of an abusive parent.

It feels like an easy parenting decision. My father didn't make that decision. His father didn't make that decision. His father . . . and so on. I suppose the first mistake is to think it is a decision at all.

My grandfather, though the memories and those who held those memories are fading fast, was also a victim. As an adult, when I asked uncles and aunts for stories about his father, my great-grandfather Bill, they did not share my nostalgia for the old man in the white undershirt, thick Clubmaster glasses and baseball cap. His direct speech and its harsh tone that I found amusing only reminded them of past cruelties. The first time my great-grandfather saw snow, he was three years old, sleeping in his bed. His father, my great-great-grandfather, Bull McGinnis, the boxer and owner of the auto-piloting donkey, thought it would be funny to pick him up, throw him into a snowbank and lock the door.

After Mexico and visiting Grandpa in North Carolina, we took the newborns to Andorra to see if such an absurd place existed. At the border they made us watch a ten-minute instructional video titled *Andorra La Majestuosa*. The film started with storm clouds gathering at time-lapse speed over the Andorran mountains. The narrator's rich deep voice in an English gilded with Catalan vowels told us, 'In 1933, foreign resident Boris Skossyreff proclaimed himself "Boris the First, King of Andorra and Regent for His Majesty the King of France" and declared war on the sovereign Bishop of Urgell, Justí Guitart i Vilardebó.' The screen showed a black-and-white photo of the would-be king. The voice-over continued to tell us that after an intense week of asking around for Skossyreff's address, the brave patriots of Andorra defeated the coup and expelled him to the hinterlands of Portugal. The photo of the defeated usurper whitewashed away. The Andorran national anthem 'El gran Carlemany' struck up and it was hard to ignore the stirrings of national pride. Yes, Andorra, yes, I thought. Between panning shots of mountains piebald with green forest and grey stone and black lakes, we watched scenes of skiers throwing out whispers of snow with each graceful swish, beautiful people with toothpaste-commercial smiles in crowded hotel bars, a small field of tobacco wedged into a valley dancing in the sun, clear and pure streams gurgling, bankers shaking hands with bearded men in thawbs lined with gold. The narrator enumerated the glories and blessings of this fine micronation ruled peacefully by two princes, the President of France and a Spanish bishop named Joan, successfully providing duty-free pleasure to 10.2 million tourists per annum and an attractive tax regime to the financial services and insurance sectors. Unfortunately, we didn't meet the salary minimums for entry so after the border guard took a clipping of hair from each of us, including the twins, he pointed us back towards France.

We drove and drove. We passed Marseille without the smallest bit of curiosity about what it would be like to live there and whether there were hills, dog shit and bad pavements that would make a reasonable-minded wheelchair user think twice before considering a move to that city. We stopped when we reached a village named Volonne. It sat beside the Durance, a languid tributary of the Rhone. A grande allée of plane trees led to a small square littered with chairs and tables next to an ancient fountain gurgling Alpine waters, where a new family could sit and drink rosé à la piscine under the screech and dart of martins and swallows. A plaque nearby commemorated the most exciting thing that happened there, which was that in March 1815 Napoleon Bonaparte stopped to relieve himself on a wall before heading north to be defeated by haemorrhoids and British-infantry tactics.

A family with three young boys lived above the one-room apartment we rented. The property was nested among apricot orchards that thickened the air with the scent of jam. In the mornings we pulled the crib outside under a wrought-iron pergola, made by the blacksmith father and thick with grapevine, to take advantage of the shade and the breeze sweeping along the river. As the twins watched the owner's naked two-year-old chase chickens, we had our breakfast of toast and the local honey while going through the basket of freshly picked fruit and vegetables left for us by the wife's morning harvest of their garden. When the summer heat had gathered its strength we took refuge in the car's AC, spending our days driving through lavender hills to nearby villages with babies snoring in the back. Each spear of purple flowers nodded with the callow fumbling of hundreds of honey-bees. Multiply the bees by the thousands and thousands of plants and the ground hummed to itself like a contented old woman. One night coming home, we followed an enormous truck overflowing with the harvest. A snow of purple swirled in our headlights and with it that divine scent.

We stayed there a month before wandering through Italy, where the girls started to ween. I thought I knew love until I saw Zed look at a green bean. Her whole body would shudder with excitement, her racoon paw of a hand snatching at it while she made a hurr hurr sound of thrill. Her eyes cross when she gets excited. Momo's younger sister has the same quirk, and I like this manifestation of inheritance whether by genetics or chance. We travelled up through northern Europe taking detours through as many micronations as possible to build up the mythology of our twins being well travelled.

The girls were in my lap as we looked at the statues of early church saints standing before the Mainz cathedral in Germany. I pointed to each, giving them their names: St Boniface, St Peter, St Paul McCartney and St T-Bone. That one was a famous wizard, I said, pointing out the staff of St Boniface, and a German passing by admonished me in English, That is not a wizard.

We found a farm owned by retired Dutch hippies on the island of Texel in the Netherlands. We rented a yurt, which is a tent but more expensive. When we checked in, they reassured us that they had already buried amethyst and tourmaline to create a protective boundary for the babies against nightmares and electromagnetic waves. They had a bike Sarah could borrow if she was careful of poles.

Poles? Like for street signs?

The Polish. They steal bikes, the woman warned. Sarah strapped the babies outward-facing to her chest and rode along the dikes, swerving any eastern Europeans she came across.

It wasn't the prevailing intra-European racism that led us to return to London. It was that the girls had become proficient and insistent crawlers. They easily and quickly zoomed beyond the antibacterial rose quartz circle. The morning that I caught Maude eating the dried husk of a wasp from underneath the dining room table, it felt time to head home.

My scars are not beautiful. They are saw-toothed atrophic marks where a transmission block seared into the meat of my arm and back. Two deep holes at my hips cut through skin and fat from where they took a bone graft to make an ersatz vertebra. The scar along my back is straight but it does not align with the battered and damaged zigzag of spine. They cut more of me out when I had osteomyelitis. The scars are violence; nothing was gained from them, only lost.

In the morning, as we slowly roused from sleep, my hand rested on the warm braid of flesh just below the curve of Sarah's belly. Once, when I told her I thought her C-section scar was beautiful, she thought I was mocking her. She took my hand away and rose to go to work. In London, with maternity leave over, our life was different.

I entertained myself by giving the twins enormous serving spoons to eat their cereal. Maude struggled to get it into the kid-sized plastic bowl and into her kid-sized mouth. For tiny people who complain about the stupidest inconsequential things, children can be extremely tolerant of their circumstances. Maude didn't complain or comment and I felt guilty for teasing her. I handed her a regular-sized spoon. She took it up and more efficiently packed Wheat-o's into her face. Meanwhile, Zed, ignoring her enormous spoon, was selecting single pieces of cereal and nibbling at them with connoisseur's diligence. Constellations of half-chewed Os surrounded her.

Outside our window I watched addicts queueing. Despite the depths of their addiction, the harm they have wrought on their bodies, etched in their faces and hands, and the distant and unseen sadness of loved ones and the personal pain that this moment marks, they were still British addicts and some mornings the queue was eight people deep. Orderly and self-organising, the spirit that coloured a quarter of the world map pink! I watched a broken-hearted Peugeot 208 pull up and the exchanges made. The dealers didn't take anything smaller than pound coins. I had seen them reject the coppers by throwing them in the face of the customer. You couldn't do that at Pret a Manger but what a disappointment it must be growing up on gangster movies where hundred-dollar bills shuffle through money counters, while these young men found themselves in a shitty hatchback smelling of mildew with a bucket of sweat-greased pound coins between their legs. After a few fights at four in the morning, break-ins and having to thread my toddlers through the inattentive human wreckage, I have grumbled and used insensitive words to describe their plight.

Zed, having noticed my attention, pointed to the window and said, Papa, you see zombies?

I wiped their faces and let them go play while I cleaned up the debris of breakfast. The wood of the dining table had grown pale under the constant scrubbing and wiping. Before I had finished the dishes, Maude's crying hit a pitch that required me to intervene. Maude wanted to sit on the twenty-four-pack of toilet paper recently delivered. Her face was scrunched and red as she pointed at Zed upon her two-ply throne.

Before I could comfort Maude, Zed told her, Lighten up, Francis. It was a quote from a Bill Murray 1980s Cold War-era film, *Stripes*. Zed only knows it as something her father says when she is play-act crying and I'm not buying it. My laughter was enough to get Maude to calm down.

A surprising amount of my parenting aphorisms come from Hollywood drill sergeants. When the girls are being unreasonable it is Gunnery Sargent Hartman from *Full Metal Jacket* that I turn to most. 'What is your major malfunction?', 'Get with the programme' or, when I'm exasperated, 'What are you trying to do to my beloved corps?'

That morning was a 'What are you two animals doing in my beloved head?' Moments after the skirmish over toilet paper, I walked in on Zed on all fours, her butt sticking in the air and Maude, delicate as a watercolourist dabbing on the last details, wiping Zed's butthole.

By the time I had everything ready – nappy bag refilled, snacks, girls dressed – the house was a disaster, but Zed had stuffed herself into a box barely big enough to fit her, her eyes devouring page after page of a book with a hunger I understood well. Maude was leaning against the raised beds in the garden, messing with the plants, playing with soil and mumbling 'Sixteen Going on Seventeen' to herself, occasionally shaking her hips to the tune in her head.

We need cake! I shouted. I wanted to celebrate this perfection.

Cake! Maude responded. Zed added, Can we have a babycino too?

Of course! Babycinos all around. Mommy's buying!

I took pride in my ability to manage two toddlers from a wheelchair. The neighbourhood aunties used to stop me to say three things: Your babies are cold. Where's mum? You're a good dad. After a few months, they shorthanded it to Good dad. I buckled the girls into my lap with a seat belt from a Vauxhall Chevette that I got from the thieves' market near Brick Lane. As a wheelchair user, I was acutely aware of topography and my route instinctively avoided steps, uneven pavement and traffic, with Maude and Zed always encouraging, go faster.

We get out of our block of flats and the junkies have cleared out except for one man who was either very late or very early for the drop-off. He noticed me but didn't move. Instead, he looked at the girls looking at him.

They're beautiful.

I'm a fan. Mind if I pass?

See you girls in eighteen years.

You'll be dead by then, I said and pushed past.

Zed asked why I was mad at the man.

I distracted her by telling them to get ready for the safety scream. When the green-man light signals it is safe to cross, we double-check that no bike or car is ignoring the red light, and then, in a calm and orderly fashion, we cross the street yelling and shouting. We are careful to point a finger at bicyclists who are being too aggressive. I have warned the girls that the most dangerous animal in London is the MAMIL, the middle-aged man in Lycra.

The place near us that does cake and babycinos was not wheelchair accessible, but they were used to the girls ordering and using the contactless pay while I stayed outside.

The girls had been on a pretty heavy *Sound of Music* jag. As we sat in front of the coffee shop, an elderly Carmelite nun walked towards us. I excitedly – maybe too much, an enthused American is hard to gauge – pointed out the nun. The girls were confused because nuns were Julie Andrews tall and twirling. The aged woman in her shapeless brown habit stopped. She didn't speak English, and I didn't speak Italian, but we chatted briefly, trading notes of admiration for my children, before she continued on her way.

That was a nun, girls! I said.

Zed said, I thought she was a junkie.

It took a few years, even after they had learned to talk, for my daughters to ask me about my wheelchair. Children don't discriminate at a fundamental level. Zed's p, d, b and q's were indistinguishable, but she unerringly knew which one she had drawn. Magic tricks too were wasted on them. Why shouldn't a little red ball disappear from my hand and appear inside an upturned cup? Shouldn't all fathers come with wheels? For several years, I was drawn without my wheelchair alongside mum and sister. I was the large stick figure with a square of black hair on the top and two green dots for eyes. When my wheelchair did appear in their drawings, I felt a twinge of regret. Not because I have any negative feelings about my wheelchair. Quite the opposite, my wheelchair is a part of me. My life would be significantly poorer without it. The feeling was the fear that the girls would see my chair first and me second, which is how it goes most of the time. The wheelchair was what the twins used to balance while learning to walk. I would lock my brakes, and they pulled themselves up. While holding on to my chair, they chased each other around Papa, giggling as I tapped them on the head as they passed. When they got older and stronger, they delighted in pushing my chair around with or without me in it. Their papa came with an extra toy.

When Zed began to understand how the wheelchair was related to my disability, she asked a lot of questions. Her focus was on the details of my accident. I've had these conversations with enough thoughtless strangers that I have my answers at the ready. She wanted to know the car's colour and why I didn't look both ways when I crossed the street. Years later, when my wife told the story of our trouble conceiving, Zed with only a basic grasp of the birds and bees looked at my wife incredulously and asked her why she hadn't tried the penis-vagina thing. Maude focused more on what I could and couldn't do as a paraplegic. There were a few weeks where she walked up steps, skipped or twirled her dress and said, You can't do this 'cause you in a wheelchair. After about a dozen of those, I lost my patience, and half-jokingly said, Well, you can't read or pour milk by yourself.

Sarah messaged: *Just landed. In taxi. See you soon.* I was eager to talk to her about the day, hoping to winkle out a sliver of anxiety I had been feeling that day.

The girls and I were sitting on the couch reading a book together when the sound of the front door being unlocked unleashed the screams of Mummy and the scrabbling rush to cling to her legs as she pulled her enormous suitcase into the living room. I went to the kitchen to get dinner ready while Sarah, like the businessmen of yore, dug through her suitcase to pull out gifts for the girls.

I picked up my phone and saw a message from my stepdad. *Momo had a heart attack.*

I told Sarah I needed to make a call before I started dinner. She sensed something was wrong, but I went to our bedroom before she could ask. Another message, *Don't be alarmed! Call me at home . . . will be here til 1pm EST*

I called my stepdad but there was no answer. I called Momo. No answer. I left messages and emails for both. Eventually, a message arrived, this time from Momo. *I am home. Feeling run over and mortal. Scary stuff. We can talk tomorrow. XOXO*

It was a day of tears. A stone marker in the flat now warns never to build below the living room unless the lamentations of my children drown your cattle. By mid-afternoon, the marble winked below the surface. Everything had been a battle: constant screaming, crying and tantrums. Tantrums because Zed wanted to go left but we needed to go right. Tantrums when we went left because she changed her mind. She teased Maude until Maude retaliated. A toddler throwing a haymaker is a sight to behold but I couldn't appreciate it then.

At the playground, Maude was crying in the swing. I ignored her to minister to Zed who had fallen. It turned out that Maude was stuck and genuinely distressed. I freed her, coating my kisses in apologies. As soon as I returned to Zed, Maude deliberately got her legs stuck again.

Sarah was back travelling for work, this time touring China. It was easier for me to manage the girls when she was away. There was no looking over the shoulder to see who was holding the parenting conch, and our relationship as a couple had disappeared below the tides. I had come to prefer it when she was travelling. I felt less lonely alone.

At dinner time, I made homemade fish fingers. The girls loved fish fingers. Their experience had been limited to store-bought bricks of processed fish that were coated in an orange that only existed in industrial food manufacturing. Sarah preferred them not to eat packaged food, and I had the clever idea to use Sarah's Christmas cookie cutters to shape my fish fingers into child-pleasing shapes. Santa's head but haddock-flavoured. I imagined my progeny shouting, Yes please, Papa!

Instead, it was more tears and fights while I cooked. A broken man delivered the dinner, but I was proud of my fish-flavoured Santa trimmed in ketchup red and mayo white. Zed, before the plate touched the table, told me she didn't like it. Maude, the more taciturn of the two, rotated the plate to carefully examine a perfect tree-shaped fish cake trimmed in garland condiments and green pea baubles. She looked at me. She looked at the fish cake. She looked at Zed sneering at hers before she cleared her throat, and in the tone and enunciation of a high court judge, asked me why I had decided to shit on a plate and set it before her. Or, she might have pushed it to the floor and cried, I don't remember.

It didn't stop after dinner. I usually intervened immediately when the girls were physical. That night, I gave up. I let them fight. I thought that when Maude saw how she had hurt her sister, she'd feel bad and never do it again. Unfortunately, according to behavioural scientists, a child does not develop empathy until four years. Maude went for Zed's eyes through a veil of red mist. I couldn't shake the disgust and anger I felt towards my daughter. By bedtime, I was racing for the finish line, a black band of unconsciousness stretched across my bed. I only had to bathe them and put them in their beds.

The bath was going well until Zed wanted to put soap in her eyes. I told her that was a bad idea. She discovered that it was indeed a bad idea. She screamed, quickly rising to hysteria. I tried to get her to wash her eyes out with her whale cup. She thrashed around, splashing Maude who had started to cry. I snatched the cup and dumped water in her face. Her hysteria hit a new pitch, blubbering about Papa. I dumped another whale-full over her head. I did it again from pique. She was yelling, Papa mean. Papa mean. I pulled her out roughly and dried her. She screamed and screeched. I pushed her out of the bathroom and closed the door to her cries. Maude, still in the bath, had stopped crying and was scared, scared of me.

The ugliness lingered in me as I laid them down. I assumed they wanted nothing to do with me, but Maude shouted 'song', in her guinea-pig squeak of a voice, from her favourite sleep position: prone with feet tucked beneath her, butt sticking up. As she settled herself, she rubbed the tops and bottoms of her feet together. They both slept like that in those first years.

I didn't grow up with lullabies, but I knew a lot of blues songs. The girls were soothed by 'Goodnight Irene' and 'Good Morning Blues' where I replaced 'Irene' and 'Blues' with the girls' names. When Maude called 'song!' as I covered her with a blanket it meant that she wanted to hear her favourite, 'Go to Sleepy, Little Baby'. I rubbed her back and sang.

To the stable we will go, to the stable we will go,
when you wake, any mule you can take

Both girls joined the refrain.

go to sleepy, little Maudie,
go to sleepy, little Zee Zee

In the dark of their room, the voice of my girls cleansed me. They held no resentment. My girls, tomorrow I will do better. Zed's voice, tinny and adorable, came from the corner of the darkened room.

Papa, you forgot to sing about the flies, she said. I had been trying to avoid the last verse now that they understood the words. I went to Zed's bed and rubbed her back.

go to sleepy, little Maudie,
go to sleepy, little Zee Zee
Buzzards and flies, picking out its eyes,
Poor little babies crying, Mamma!

I went to bed, but my heart began that triple beat that sent me to the hospital in Germany. I thought I was going to die, and my imagination followed my toddlers finding my corpse and the two days that followed until the cleaner let herself into the flat. My heart pounded as my veins spit out adrenalin. Blood pumped in my ears with a tscht tscht tscht as I took deep breaths.

When we first lived together, Sarah regularly dreamed about me dying in horrible baroque ways. New in our relationship, I wondered if this was partly hopeful. Her life would be better if I died. At twenty, she had fallen in love with a boy who would be a cripple for the rest of his life. There were dozens of other boys, whole and undamaged, who required no logistics and care. On a whim, these boys could do anything, go anywhere. There would be no need for phone calls in advance to check access. No disappointments when finding that accessibility is in the eye of the beholder. Sarah could skip those first months where the only outing I could manage was a wander around the neighbourhood counting cats until the painkillers stopped working. Now I understand Sarah's nightmares were something different. She loved me. Her biggest fear was losing me and she almost had.

After a few minutes, I calmed myself, and left the deadbolt unlocked because Zed and Maude knew how to open the bottom lock. In my morbid scenario, they would go to the flat above and tell the neighbours, Papa won't wake up.

I was awakened by a sound, maybe, retching. I lay in the dark to understand if it was in my dream or not. Was the noise from outside? Maybe it was a crunching noise? Someone breaking in again? Addicts fighting in the street? My ears scanned the static of silence. There, that was it. Smaller, quieter that time, but that was it.

It was one of the girls.

I transferred over, unlocked my wheels and went to their room navigating by the streetlights coming through windows. Zed had been sick. She was sitting up, holding her mouth. Her pyjamas were a mess. The sheets too. I scooped her up and brought her to the bathroom. Maude hadn't stirred at all. Asleep and sucking her thumb. Her bare feet tucked and crossed beneath her bottom.

Zed vomited again, a chartreuse of bile streaked with ribbons of blood as I stripped her down and cleaned her up. I put her in my bed with a couple of plastic bowls on the nightstand just in case. I filled a sippy cup with some water but asked her to wait until her stomach was settled before she tried to drink. The thin offerings of green and yellow kept coming up and with it, brown granules that an internet search told me were digested blood. By two a.m., I woke Maude. I wanted to have everything ready when the ambulance arrived. I packed the extra clothes, snacks and toys we would need for a night at the A & E. At the last minute I grabbed the travel pram.

The paramedics arrived with a quiet professional surety that put me at ease. Even the added complication of a paraplegic, his wheelchair and a healthy twin didn't delay us much. The girls gawped at the spaceship-like interior of the ambulance's stark white cabinets, coloured instruments and promising backlit buttons that I pretended to push.

No, papa, Maude squealing. While Zed's vitals were taken, she watched the tower blocks swirl with silent blue lights as we sped to the hospital.

As we waited in triage for a bed, the 24-hour news channel cycled through video clips of a war with wide rubble-strewn streets stretched between bullet-chewed buildings. When they cut to screaming, bloodied children, I used my phone to spoof the remote and changed it to something more kid friendly. Sumo wrestling on Eurosport was as good as it got.

Zed, holding a bedpan at the ready, was a slump of heartbreaking weight on my lap. I rubbed her head and kissed her ear.

You're doing good, you're so brave, I whispered. The doctor is going to take care of you.

I'm tired, Papa.

Maude, not tired at all, busied herself in the corner at that table all waiting rooms have, where the child threads square beads through a three-dimensional zigzag of intertwining wires. Nearby, a girl in a headscarf and her mother stared at the television. I couldn't tell which was the patient. A promising first-division young Samoan tossed salt as he entered the ring. The women didn't seem to notice or care that I changed the channel.

Another woman at the end of the room was talking to her ghosts in a mix of English and French. Most often I heard her saying 'sorry' in the two languages. She was well dressed, her grey hair washed and styled. The make-up was a lurid red for the lips and a bright blue for the eyelids. Her eyes swam among the unseeable things in the room. From a Waitrose bag-for-life, she withdrew a screw-cap white wine and took purposeful draws.

Distracted by a controversy over the Samoan winning the match despite his foot being first outside, I didn't notice that the woman had moved next to me until I smelled her soap and shampoo.

She searched my face. Her brows knitted and relaxed,

knitted and relaxed. She was struggling with something, but I couldn't help her.

Sorry, Sorry. Desolé. Despite the jumble of languages, I understood she wanted to know why I was in a wheelchair.

It doesn't matter, I said and stared back, hoping to cow the conversation.

Sorry, Sorry. Desolé.

Her tight smile became a frown, and she returned to her end of the room, glowering and repeating apologies.

By the time they had a bed and a diagnosis for Zed, my phone had died. She had torn the lining in her oesophagus and the bleeding was causing the constant vomiting which was exacerbating the wound. She was given some medicine and managed to keep water down, but they wanted to keep her overnight for observation, concerned by her dehydration and an arrhythmia that they wanted to monitor. They had a bed available upstairs in the paediatric unit. They told me I could stay with her overnight, but someone would have to pick up Maude. I explained that my wife was in China. We have no family here. My phone was dead. Panic crept into my voice. I hadn't been able to get Maude to sleep in the pram and she had reached the psychosis of an overtired small child. The nurse went to see what could be done.

Zed patted my hand. Hers seemed tinier than usual. The little, perfect fingers appeared from a square of medical tape and tubing. Even when they had put in a cannula, she hadn't complained.

Don't cry, Papa. Be brave.

I laughed and kissed my beautiful daughter.

Maude mimicked her, Be brave, Papa, and I kissed my other beautiful daughter.

The doctor came to our bedside with the nurse.

They could not allow a non-patient to be in the hospital overnight, that's the policy. However, Maude could be admitted too but prescribed no treatment. The problem was that they didn't have a spare bed.

I have the pram, I said.

They brought us up to our room and we settled in. The doctor even lent me his phone charger. I turned out the lights, tucked in the girls and tried to get myself comfortable by sitting in the visitor chair and putting my feet into my wheelchair. It was not comfortable, and I didn't sleep. From the dark, Zed asked if I could sing again.

Go to sleepy, little Maudie,
Go to sleepy, little Zee Zee

Sarah was in Japan for two and a half weeks. The girls had been easy, we had our routine, but I felt anxious all day. Parenting is to have a thousand little niggling worries and fears as you protect the most important people in your life and who are completely disinterested in self-preservation. I had meant to check on Momo, but I lost track of time and was rushing to get the girls to their swim lesson.

In the changing room of the Victorian public pool, each cubicle had a tiled bench behind a flimsy door constantly rattled by frantic mothers managing newborns, towels and Yoyo travel prams. In the corner, the fermenting nappy bin added its sour notes to the humid air. Children took advantage of the few seconds of freedom between changes to piss on the floor, and parents had been varied in their diligence in mopping up spills. Happily, I had the key to the disabled changing room, a clean, fresh-smelling refuge, larger than our bedroom in the flat. Maude and Zed battled for the pool wheelchair, a contraption of PVC tubing and plastic wheels they use to deliver the non-ambulatory to the pool. Maude loved swim class mostly because she got to wear her swimsuit with the dolphin on the chest and matching swim cap. She stared at us through her goggles as I argued with Zed, who refused to go swimming. I told her she had to put on her suit and whether she swam was up to her.

The swim instructor waded in the pool dressed in shorts and T-shirt in the waist-high water. As soon as she raised her arms for Zed to come to the poolside, my daughter exploded into tears and hysterics. This was happening every week. When I asked my aunt for advice, she had none. Her adult daughter still couldn't swim. Grandma told me that Grandpa threw Dad off a dock and that's how he learned, which might explain my aunt's laissez-faire approach to her children's swim education.

I tried to point out how much fun her sister was having, but Zed insisted that she could already swim.

Holding on to Mommy is not swimming, I said, but I gave up and returned my attention to Maude who was pulling herself out of the water. She shivered, holding her fists to her chest as she watched the bigger children doing laps. As soon as they were on the other side of the pool she jumped in and time jittered. The seconds from her jumping until she was submerged became years.

It is an adult woman who returns to the surface. For a moment I think that it is Sarah in the water. That adult Maude is an exact copy of Sarah when she was a young woman. As I watch the woman's arms rise above and fall with each stroke, I have a sense of the woman she is, will be, could be. I have found her in a moment, at some point in the future where she is afraid for me. I have hurt myself or am ill. It's a sense more than an understanding. I'm an older dad. In the instant it takes to crush a spine twenty years were lopped off the end of my life. I might not get to see my daughter as this adult woman. That thought ripped me back to my little girl 'shark swimming'. She had made a fin with her hands at the top of her head and was kicking towards a coveted pink pool noodle. A little boy in a Nemo body suit tried to take it away from her but, with a ninja flick of water into his eyes, she swam away with the prize.

At the end of the thirty-minute session, I wrapped Maude in her terry-cloth ladybird with its two terry-cloth legs dragging behind. I kissed her and said how proud I was. A huge smile burst from her, and she demonstrated the 'shark swim' form and asked if I saw her kicking her legs. Yes, yes, yes.

Let's go, I said to Zed, but she refused to leave. She wanted to stay and watch the next class.

You can't swim in that one. It's for older kids, I said. She ignored me.

Can I swim with you? Zed asked.

Not today, I didn't bring my suit. The truth was that I once tried to take the girls swimming on my own, but a lifeguard told me in front of my kids that it wasn't safe for just me to go in with them. Whether he was right or wrong, the shame checked me.

Sarah had a few months when she wasn't away for work, but we were still not in the same place. She still had to commute three hours a day, starting early and finishing late. Each night I had dinner with the girls. No custom-made meals, now. The golden rule of feeding small children: if it is brown, it'll go down. Still, each night, I haggled with Zed over the definition of eating 'all' your vegetables as I cleared Maude's ear holes of sweet potato. They were bathed, in their pyjamas and asleep by the time Sarah got home. As soon as she did, I made her a plate of the leftovers, and I left to go finish my novel in a doughnut shop on Brick Lane. The only time we spoke was after I came home and got into bed.

Remember the lady, the other one with twins, I said, transferring from my wheelchair to the bed and getting undressed.

The weird-looking twins with curly hair?

Yeah, like little aliens in Harpo wigs.

Cute though. Not many can pull off that look.

Not even Harpo himself, I said. I turned off my phone. I didn't need an alarm. Maude would be waking us up in less than five hours.

I thought you were working.

I was. Then I stopped at the pub to do my emails.

To get the nightly divorce report from the monkey family.

I didn't respond. I put on my eye mask, a freebee from one of her business trips. Last month, when I was freshly showered after being covered in an explosion of bright orange liquid shit, Sarah sent me a selfie from a first-class seat captioned, 'free upgrade!' It wasn't that we weren't communicating. We were living in two different worlds, speaking in different languages.

Single mum. Twins. I can't imagine, she said to herself.

Huh? I asked, taking off the hi-vis earmuffs I had been using to block out the dawn chorus of the girls shouting for Mummy.

She asked, Do you know what happened?

Twins, right? Three years, no help, no childcare. I only saw the husband on the weekends, always on his phone.

After the doughnut shop closed, I had been going to a pub to do the freelance work that I hadn't finished during the girls' nap time. At closing, the doughnut shop gave me the unsold stock, which I offered to the pub regulars, a mix of career alcoholics in various stages of their addictions. I had been joining them and leaving my copyedits for yet another tomorrow.

It was an old Irish pub with draped tricolours, photos of footballers with massive sideburns, and a wall of antique Guinness beer-tap handles, one of which fell when the heavy front doors were slammed.

Reigning over the confederacy of drunks was a cockney

family: father, mother, adult brother, adult sister and their pet orangutan, Kevin. They ran a well-known company that built theatre sets for West End productions. I don't think Kevin had any actual responsibilities in the business, but he was very presentable in his red kickers, nappy and a child's bomber jacket with the company logo on the back. He patiently nursed a Pernod and black, while the family downed their pints. His one task, in which he took great delight, was to reset the tap handle onto the wall after admonishingly brandishing it at the patron whose door slam had made it fall. On rare occasions, Kevin investigated my jacket buttons with his prehensile lips, emptied my pockets or intensely searched my eyes. Each interaction with Kevin felt as if I had chanced upon a primordial forest spirit not quite ready for his night out at a Stone Roses gig. Mostly though, he spent the night sipping at his drink and cuddling the mum with the occasional whiff of ape shit to remind me of the weirdness of the situation. Despite Kevin's support for Watford FC, which no one explained, everyone treated his existence in the pub as unremarkable.

That night I had brought matcha donuts which the sister handed over to Kevin; he only liked the matcha ones. I sat between her and a guy who had had a minor synth-pop hit in the early eighties. The only thing he had left from that success was the haircut. He was diabetic and we all politely ignored that he was drinking himself to death. He had moved to the neighbourhood from Goa in the seventies, pulled to London along with the receding tide of hippy tourists. We were listening to Kevin's dad bitching about how all the flats in his building were short-term lets. Key boxes lintelled the entrance. The pop star sighed and reminded him of the Bethnal Green where racketeers knocked at their studio, the night he watched from his window as a drunk lit his cigarette off a burning car, and of the pub round the corner, now a ramen bar, that used to fly National Front flags. That killed the mood for complaining about gentrification, so the sister solicited compliments for her haircut. The best I could manage was that it suited her eyes while Kevin picked neon-green flecks of icing from his arm hair, nibbling at them as if they were nits. At the other end of the pub the alien twins' dad had come in with a woman and the mum mentioned the divorce. Everyone, even Kevin, turned their head at the same time as Kevin's mum told us about him being thrown out of the flat.

Before our daughters were born, I would have told Sarah about how Kevin had grown restless and frisbee-ed a beer coaster to the bartender. His dad reprimanded him – 'leave it out, Kevin' – to which the orangutan retorted with an impatient huff. We would have laughed about it together. Instead, as soon as I lay down next to her, I told her about the alien twins' parents and their divorce.

On Wednesdays, I called my dad when the twins were at nursery. I don't know if it was becoming a grandparent, or fortuitous timing that Sarah and I became parents when he had found enough serenity to seal the mouths of his ghosts, but he had become present in a new way. Mostly our conversations were the superficial chit-chat between strangers who happen to share a last name, but I understood that it takes time to rebuild upon land harried and burned, regardless of how long ago.

Can I ask you something? I asked.

Sure, what d'ya got for me? he replied. His background was set to an open-plan office of concrete and exposed piping with a city skyline beyond the large windows. The scene rippled when he moved like the pixelated vapour that it was.

I told him that since Sarah went back to work my drinking had tipped over into something unhelpful, a novel and unwelcome needfulness to dull the edges of anxiety, exhaustion and loneliness. I suggested that I understood how addictions began. The sharp points of life dulled for a moment. I was looking for insight, maybe confirmation, from this man, my father, who had lost so much to addiction, but as I spoke my ridiculous presumption struck me. I knew nothing. I understood nothing. My problem was I had no problems. Dad immediately and swiftly moved the conversation elsewhere and I hid away my trifle, saving us from embarrassing myself further.

The twins, in the full flush of toddler psychopathy, were attacking each other regularly and I wasn't handling it well. Anger lingered in me against my daughters who were too young to understand. It didn't take Alice Miller to get why I would have a hypersensitivity to a child being hit, even if by another child. The fights were a daily occurrence and, one Saturday afternoon, Maude scratched at Zed's face, drawing blood. Zed's howls brought Sarah running into the room where she saw me yanking Maude from her sister. She flew back, fell and hit her head on the table. Both girls crying now, and Maude was screaming 'Papa hurt me' over and over. I tried to leave the room to gain control but the fear on Sarah's face helped turn the disgust I felt on to her.

What did you do to her? she demanded.

The clean burn of our anger made it easy to ignore the ugliness that poured out and puddled at our feet while our daughters screamed and howled forgotten in the melee. Sarah moved out of my way when I told her I preferred it when she was away. It was easier to parent and less lonely.

Kevin and his family were in the pub when I arrived that night. The crying, the yelling, Sarah and the girls and most of all the guilt faded away as soon as I pulled up next to the sister. She had been getting flirty lately. She was interested in writing or being a writer, which are not the same, and we talked about that. With a book deal, I could pretend I had something to say on the subject. She had round and full lips, almost too much, so her mouth was never quite closed. She had a habit of pulling out a cigarette long before she announced she was going for a smoke. I didn't smoke but this time I followed.

She announced she was going to sit on my lap. Okay, I said. She put her arm around me as we chatted. The mix of cigarette, her too-sweet perfume and the sweaty, too-human musk of Kevin on her was not completely unpleasant. My hand that I was awkwardly holding down and away, I rested on her knee. She blew smoke above our heads. She picked a loose Kevin hair from her jumper. I tried and failed not to look at her tits.

When we returned, the dad asked Kevin with a knowing smile what he thought the kids were talking about out there. Shut it, the sister said. I pretended not to hear. While I watched Kevin lift the brother's nose to inspect his nostrils, a drunk passed the table and bumped into me. I hadn't locked my brakes, so I was shoved into the table and spilled our fresh pints. The dad snapped his fingers to get the bartender's attention and shouted, Ginger Twat Tim is back. Oi, Ginger Twat Tim, out. Fuck off, Ginger Twat Tim, the bar chorused.

When I came home, Zed said Mummy was crying.

I went to our bedroom. Sarah was lying down with her back to me.

Kevin's brother is getting divorced, I said.

That isn't going to happen to us, she said.

I told her the story. They were together since they were twenty, like us. They had a ten-year-old boy together. Over the years, they had forgotten to be a couple. The only things they did together were birthday parties, recitals and lunches with other parents. They had no shared interests, which at first was bothersome until it wasn't. Then it didn't matter. They both had busy jobs, but they were good parents. That felt enough. But it wasn't, was it? Then some woman at one of the theatres they work with flirted with him and he flirted back. I don't know if that was true. His exact words had been, And I started fucking around.

A month went by and nothing changed, because there was work and commuting and unreasonable toddlers that woke us up at four or five in the morning. One night I came home directly from the doughnut shop. I lay down beside Sarah. I put my hand on her hip. She was reading a book. I kissed her, breathed her scent and rested my head against her shoulder. No response. I got up and left the flat.

In the pub, the weight of the mood was immediately felt. The family had been fighting with the council to keep Kevin. He had his own room and everything. He'd been with the family his entire life. Everyone knew Bethnal Green Kevin in his kickers with his Pernod and blacks, but the path of appeals had come to an end. London Zoo was coming to take him in the next few days. Kevin was particularly clingy that night, moving from person to person to push his head beneath theirs and wrap his impossibly long arms around them. He gave me a pat on the head, and I took it as a thank you for all the doughnuts. The regulars gathered around the family to commiserate and listen to Kevin stories. I was sitting next to the sister. As we worked through the rounds, her eyes lingered longer as did the press of her shoulder against mine. As closing time approached, the discussion came around to going to Kevin's house and continuing the leaving do.

The daughter leaned in and kissed my neck before

commanding, Come with. I looked at the scene around me. The dad's face was flushed and puffy with drink. Kevin pressed against his weeping mother, patting her head. The elbows of my jumper were damp from spilled beer. I imagined us back at her flat in her room. She unsteadily pulling off her top for me to see the body that I had been imagining, to claim that prize, as I lay in her bed against the spin of drink. The years of being ignored, and undesired, no matter how understandable, gave me my reason. Generations of men had made this decision with little to no consequences. To have the heat of another's body against mine, however fleeting, however disappointing, with a drunk orangutan snoring beneath his Watford FC duvet in the next room. That was what I wanted. I leaned in for her to kiss my neck again. She complied. This could happen. She drew back to look at me, suddenly shy and embarrassed at her suggestion.

I would have said, Yes. I would have ruined everything at that moment. The once in a lifetime history Sarah and I had built together over twenty years would have burned as quickly as tissue. Never mind the uncertainty and pain I would have caused my young daughters. It scares me to think what I would have lost and that it was saved not because I made the right choices. I had not been making the right choices for a while now. My beautiful life today is because a jerk with a pit bull came into the pub and asked if they were still serving.

The bartender said no. The man slid in and said, Just a sneaky half, then. A square-headed black dog lumbered in behind him. As the man argued with the bartender, the dog and Kevin locked eyes. The dog went nuts and the men shouted over the growing noise. Kevin clung to the mum, baring his teeth and pointing at the dog. The argument became about the dog. You can't have a dog in here. No dogs allowed. They have a monkey. Someone shouted the correction, Great ape, and the expected laughter followed. Kevin became more and more agitated. He pointed at the loose tap handle and the mum said no. The dad got up. He approached the guy, ignoring the dog, and calmly stated that it would be best for him and his dog if he left. The man stood braced against the fierce tug of the lead. The dad tried to explain that it was a going-away party for his son and his presence was an intrusion. To me, the dad was always a jovial cockney-geezer type, but it was hard not to notice his size and demeanour at that moment. The man with the dog hesitated for a moment but recovered his bravado. He told the dad to go fuck himself, his son and his damn dirty ape. The man only managed a smug grin, pleased with his film reference, before the dad slammed the front door shut and swung it wide open again. Kevin caught the tap handle in midair. In a ginger blur and a yelp, Kevin clubbed the pit bull and flung it out of the pub as if it were a plushie. By the time we all poured out of the pub, Kevin was riding the dog, disappearing around the fried chicken shop at the corner with the man running after. Moments later, Kevin returned. Can apes swagger? Kevin did. He handed the tap handle to the mum like a repentant gunslinger and climbed up her for a cuddle. In the chaos and chatter, I slipped away and home.

I passed through the estate. It was silent and still. Only a few kitchen lights remained but the spice of home cooking still hung between the buildings. When I got to our block of flats, I vomited and up came all the beer, the shots, the doughnuts, the rottenness of those past months. I smelled the BO and shit of Kevin and the sickly perfume of the daughter. And it started again and again until I tasted a last weak trickle of bile as I tried not to get it on my shoes and wheelchair.

When I entered the flat, I washed my face in the kitchen sink. I washed my neck too as if her kisses had left a stain. I threw out the stinking jumper. Sarah was still in bed reading. I apologised and told her we needed to talk.

Do you have another divorce story for me from the monkey family?

No. No more divorces for the monkey family.

Momo

A boy. He is two. He stands in the backyard of a small white house in Clovis, New Mexico. He is fixed in this moment and nowhere else. The brown husks of autumn leaves spider among the desert's scrub bushes. He holds a cookie. The wind tussles his black curls. Unnoticed by him, his mother steps to the glass sliding door and cries. She sees not the boy but the man he will be. He will grow up. He will move away. He'll become this man she sees who will love a woman other than her, will become a father, move further and further away. She knows too her husband will leave or she will leave him. Her mother will die in the next few years as her father did when she was a girl. Her fear of dying alone echoes from fifty years in the future.

The little boy senses his mother, turns, smiles and runs to her.

It is rare that Momo phones. Before she said hello, she said, You ass.

What? I asked.

I opened your package.

What package?

The hair.

I had shaved my head. I'm always surprised at how black my hair is, and Sarah is always slightly annoyed about how surprised I am.

Yes, yes, it's blue-black. Throw it away, she had said when I showed her the dustpan.

Family photo albums are spotted with old Polaroids and even older black-and-white brownie-box camera shots of my dad, grandpa, uncles and cousins with baroque combinations of sideburns, moustaches and beards. Facial topiarism runs in the family. When we first moved to London, I wanted a style I remembered seeing in a black-and-white movie. The only example I could find was a propaganda poster of a jutting chinned, blond Deutsche student from the thirties. I was after his side part and clean taper fade, not the murderous politics. I didn't think anything of it, but in the appointment book I was written down as 'The Hitler Guy'.

It seemed a shame to just throw out my hair, and Momo's dog had been going bald. So, I put the hair into a box with a tube of superglue and a nice little card that the girls decorated. On the reverse, the card said, '(small) Dog Patch Kit', with instructions on how to fill in the dog's bald spots with my hair clippings. Momo had received the package and had only thought of how her lovely son, her only child, had mailed her a surprise gift.

When I opened it, I screamed, she said. I thought you had been kidnapped and the next box I'd get would have your toes in it.

Hearing Momo's deep, unmistakable voice and my laughter, the twins arrived to investigate. I was on the couch with my legs in my wheelchair. The neuropathic pain lessens with my feet elevated. The girls climbed into my nook to play with the video filters. That day's filter was a pug puppy. The girls took turns making faces to watch the pug in the corner of the screen copy them. The pug on the screen with Momo's lips told me she called because she had to tell me that, last night, she felt someone tugging her awake and she thought it was her husband.

I woke up and it was my mom standing over me, she said.

Maude's pug lips moved to say, Is Momo's mom alive?

What did you do? I asked Momo.

She was wearing the last outfit I saw her in, a white T-shirt and plain slacks. My heart was pounding. She said she had seen her great-grandchildren. She said how beautiful they were, and I said, Yes, they are. She asked if they were good girls. I said, Yes, they are.

Who said we were good girls? Maude wanted to know.

I said, Let me talk to Momo for a second.

Momo continued, We talked about you. She was proud of you too. The last thing she said was she had to go but she would see me soon.

Are you okay, I asked, thinking about her recent heart attack.

No, my heart was pounding the whole time. I thought she was going to take me away then and there.

No, I mean. Did you hear something from the cardiologist?

No, no, no. At my age, there's always something falling off, but the cardiologist is happy with the dosage I'm on. I'm just tired all the time.

That's scary.

Tell me about it. The last time that happened to me was after my dad died. I woke up to him sitting on the edge of my bed like he was checking on me. I saw the indentation of him. I felt a hand on my leg and then he left.

After the phone call, Maude was asking questions. Words are harder for her than for Zed. The thoughts are there but they take a little longer to marshal and march in the same direction. I try to be patient and entreat Zed to give her a chance.

Is Momo's mom alive?

No.

But she talked to her.

She had a dream that she talked to her.

Is Momo going to die?

No, I hope not. I like talking to her. Do you like talking to her? Not many people have a pug for a grandma.

Maude laughs often and easily. It is one of the easy joys in my life. I remember the first time she laughed. I was pretending to be a cat puking on her. I stole that bit from Graham Norton when he did it to Natalie Portman on his show.

Years before the twins were born, I returned to Florida from London for the occasion of Momo's graduation. Nearing retirement, she returned to school to finish her bachelor's degree, not because it would improve her job prospects or give her something to do in the evenings, but because it was something left undone, having dropped out to be a wife and mother. A long but direct flight over an ocean that divides the halves of the life I have lived.

The house that she and my stepdad lived in always had one more couch or chair than was reasonable for the room. The surfeit of furniture is my stepdad's, taken in place of payment. He gave most people one more chance beyond what's considered reasonable. It was how he paid back the people that gave him that one extra chance, the one in which he was redeemed. When driving through my hometown, he pointed out the bars and bottle clubs that he was thrown out of during his days of addiction. It takes a lot to be barred from a Florida bottle club, but knowing my stepdad sober, I can imagine that with whiskey and cocaine, he was up to the challenge. On the coffee table between Momo and me, there is a 1:8 scale Pocher Rolls-Royce model car. Apparently, it was once worth money, but over the decades it has fallen to pieces like a desert carcass. Its gradual dissolution held within a broken case has measured the time since I had moved out.

From our couches, we heard the snores, stuttering breath, and the occasional wet snort of an obese pug, Hogan, named for a famous golfer. The resonating bones of his skull and muffling plica of fur rendered the sound non-directional, as if the house had sinusitis. The TV, as always, was tuned to a horror movie. Momo only reads and watches horror. A habit from childhood. She has explained that it was her escape, that it was a comfort that there was somewhere worse, scarier, than her home. As zombie dinosaur fossils terrorised bikini girls, Momo and I planned the playlist for her funeral. I was not giving it my full attention. Let's blame the dog, and the always-on-always-too-loud TV, and that we have planned her funeral many times.

She was a young mother, barely in her twenties when I was born, and we grew up together. My childhood memories are filled with games she invented. The napkins in my lunchbox always had her drawings and notes. I still have one of Jabba the Hutt with a speech bubble saying, Have a good day and behave. There were the years that we lived side by side under my father's unpredictable rule. We survived the collision of her first sober days and my teenage years. Where my relationship with Dad has required diligence, with Momo it is an aged friendship worn smooth. We have decades of shared experiences to laugh, tease and talk over. We meandered from the funeral playlist to her wanting to know if she was a good parent. I turned away from the bad CGI TV death to look at her. I reassured her that she was a good mom. We have had this conversation many times as well, but I made sure to listen as she apologised for not knowing any better and not protecting me enough. I absolve her every time because parenting is always the guilt and fear that you should have known better.

I've never retained her funeral playlist, none of the permutations. The songs on that list would have shown the shifts and changes in Momo through the years. With her list, she is communicating something about us, about her. 'Forever Young' by Rod Stewart is on there. Every time we made the list that song was mentioned. The only thing the song conjures for me is the creeps I felt as a kid watching a shoulder-padded Rod Stewart singing and holding a rental ginger child, but she never appreciates this opinion. At some point, I inevitably teased her with inappropriate suggestions.

What about 'Ass N Titties' by DJ Assault as mourners took their seats among the pews?

She will have brandished her usual threat: You do, and I'll come back and haunt you.

Earlier that day, I had picked her up for a celebratory graduation lunch and paraded her around town. I had rented a convertible banana-yellow Mustang. She was beaming as we drove around St Armand's Circle, a large roundabout surrounded by pricey restaurants, art galleries and other expensive shops for the wealthy, elderly tourists that Sarasota attracts. She was enjoying the showing off. As I drove around the circle, I put on DJ Assault's magnum opus. She ducked down, yelling for me to turn it off, slapping at my seat, but grinning the entire time.

Momo's father died in his forties, not much older than I am now – an insurance salesman who held no policy himself and left the family in debt. The liquor store bill alone was in the hundreds. Her cirrhotic mother was forced to try and support a family of four children as a lunch lady. She died at fifty-six. When Momo had outlived the age her parents reached, she called to tell me. It was a milestone that needed to be shared.

Over the years, we've both treated her death lightly. When the conversation across the couches moved from the playlist to her half-serious taunts that she would be dead before Sarah and I decided to have kids, I teased back. I assured her that even in death she would be part of our future children's lives. I told her how her corpse would be stuffed like a hunting lodge bear: clawed hands raised, face fixed with menace and red LEDs for eyes. Her taxidermy would be kept in a hall closet. Whenever our children mis-behaved, we would threaten them with a visit to Grand-ma's. She loved that idea. She has a great laugh, deep and full – by phone, she is addressed as 'sir' – cured by over a half-century of being a diligent smoker of menthols. The next day at work she bragged about her imagined grand-children screaming, No! Don't put me in the closet with Grandma!

There are limits to our gallows humour though. The borders are never clear until crossed. I cannot joke about the movie *Human Centipede*, because in tears she told me, that kind of thing really happens to people. She often muses, with a trace of pride, that all the horror books she has read will come to haunt her in dementia. It is okay though to joke about her retirement plan being a coconut cream pie, a bottle of seltzer and a long one-way walk into a forest.

The fate of her remains cannot be made light of. It must be cremation. She has a phobia about being buried alive. In our many conversations about her funeral, she pauses the banter to seriously discuss her terror of waking up in the total blackness of an interred coffin. Each time I must assure her that I will make sure she is dead dead. How I do this is never discussed, but I cannot make jokes. Once she is confident that this wish will be respected, we go back to the filigrees of her funeral. The plan to pack her casket with coconut, glitter and fireworks to shower the crematorium's gathered mourners always meets with her approval. The smell of toasted coconut is a favourite of hers.

The playlist is lost but this moment sticks with me as the first time I saw her as old and thought of her as mortal. She had stopped dying her thick black hair a long time ago. The silver-white of it suits her and adds to the witchiness. The fierce green of her eyes is well nested in the wrinkles and leather of a lifetime smoker. We all have that moment when we realise that our parents have become old. The memory of them at the height of their strength is replaced with this elderly simulacrum. It is a single moment, and it is tinged with resentment. A switch begrudgingly flipped as the parent steps out of the car visiting you at college or as you return home after being away in the UK for several years. It is a moment that comes with embarrassment too as if you've discovered their secret. That they are not the all-knowing and ever-protecting parent. They are fallible and mortal. Maybe under it all, it is the realisation that after they are gone, you're next.

I sometimes worry Momo's fixation on death is wistful. She attempted suicide at least once. One night, she, in the words of AA, finally got sick and tired of being sick and tired. She told me years later that despite the abuse, the other women, the drinking, the fear and uncertainty, it was Dad who left her. She had torn through all the alcohol in the house and moved on to pulling off the atomisers of her perfume bottles, wincing through shot after shot until her bathroom sink was full of their emptied irregular shapes. She riffled through Dad's closet and found his thirty-two. A long-barrelled, lean revolver. It's not clear to me whether she pulled the trigger or not. She said no. She also said that Dad told her later that he had removed the sear from the pistol years ago lest his curious son hurt himself. She wouldn't have figured out the pistol was inoperable unless she had felt the trigger fall back without its snapping resistance and without the shot firing. She told me that sitting there on the floor, gun in her lap, that it was the thought of me that stopped her. That she couldn't bear the damage her self-destruction would wreak on her troubled son. She felt afresh the pain her parents had nested inside her so many decades ago.

She had not protected me enough, but she would not be the cause of pain.

I couldn't do to you what they did to me, she has said.

There on the floor of her bedroom, she saw the clean simplicity of death and she chose to endure what at the time was unendurable. Life is complicated and unrelenting until it isn't. Death is easy. Life is harder than death. I understand this. It scares me how much.

That moment looking at my babies' feet when I broke down crying, hoping it was me, my generation of father, who stopped the perennial child abuse: that wasn't true. It was my mom. She did it, not me. That scared and abused little girl, with no emotional tools or support, flung from an abusive home to an abusive marriage, somehow, through her principal instinct as a parent, gave me the safety and certainty to grow up intact enough to be the man, the husband and the father that I am. I can't repay my mom for that, but I can pause our banter when she apologises for the past. The only thing I can do is to remind her she was and is the best mom.

Over the years her health has declined. She still smokes and drinks nothing but coffee, while wondering aloud what might be causing her insomnia. I should be more conscientious about getting her to eat better, and quit the cigs and coffee, but it wouldn't change anything. After the twins were born, our conversations have been almost every other day, more so since her husband passed away. The girls are old enough to call Momo on their own. Maude will take my phone into her room, and I hear them talking. Zed and Momo talk about what books they are reading.

Sometimes I call when the girls are not home to talk without child-sized interruptions. After her death, I will inevitably chastise myself that I could have done more for her and spoken more often. Right now, she is here. She endures. She still very much lives her life. Forcibly retired, she works part-time at the mall. She tells me that she likes to arrive an hour early for her shift to sit near the winding lines of children waiting for Santa, revelling in the toddling chaos, snatching overheard absurdities and malapropisms, and thinking of her grandchildren. The dead will never show me her home. The impossibility of a premonition of her death is right beside its ever-presence in my fears. The full weight of mourning her cannot be borne until it must be.

For years, I felt my father's death was imminent. I knew that if my aunt or grandma called, it was about my father and it was never good news. I have written my father's eulogy on several occasions. These drafts are the lines marking the high tide of my concern, but he has luck that a nine-lived cat would envy. Those unfinished sketches of my feelings for him will never be read at a service. I don't know what I'd say at his funeral, but I've had dreams that I think are about his death. It makes me afraid. The other day he messaged to say thanks for a Christmas card we had sent. He mentioned a doctor's visit and being sent for a blood test. I immediately messaged back. The tests were routine. There was nothing to worry about.

My premature eulogies remain in the OS equivalent of a desk drawer, a reminder of the worry and concern I have felt for him for decades. Despite a hardness I've cultivated, maybe even learned from him, I love my dad and will miss him, especially these days when there seems a chance that we might have a relationship I haven't known since I was a child sitting under a tree, in the last house that had any happiness for us as a family. In the shared family nomenclature, it is known as the 'River House', because it was on a quarter-acre of the Pithlachascotee River, better known to locals as the Cootie. We canoed its length and dived its brackish depth heedless of alligators. Beneath an oak thick and greyed by beards of Spanish moss, the river's placid black waters in front of us, Dad held a handful of leaves. He pinched between his thumb and finger two smaller leaves, rich green on one side, dusty silver on the other. He told me they were hydrogen and hydrogen atoms liked hanging out together in pairs. If you add an oxygen atom, he said. He took a large leaf and put it between the two small ones. That is water, two hydrogen atoms and one oxygen, H two O. Do you know hydrogen peroxide?

I knew it well and fondly recalled its satisfying astringent smell and the bubbling foam from the many cuts and scrapes a boy growing up on a Florida river receives.

Well, that was just H two O two. He added another large leaf to his hand adjusting them to match the chemical structure of the molecule.

The next time I talked to Momo on the phone, I asked about Grandpa. We spoke about the time we took the babies to North Carolina. As we played cards, Grandpa had sniped and teased Dad who had smiled inscrutably under the barrage. I didn't understand the antagonism. Even if it wasn't done in mean-spiritedness, it was embarrassing. Dad's patience was admirable. Did Dad have a unique understanding of Grandpa and his abuse? Is it because he knows the importance of forgiving the past to do right today? Did his continued contact with Grandpa put the ghosts of the past to rest? And whose ghosts? Or was it a way of keeping them around to haunt and vex them both further?

Mostly, I enjoyed their company. I wondered why we pretend that everything that happened is forgotten.

Momo said, But we are not pretending anything. The past is only a burden if you insist on carrying it into the present.

Despite looking like a human roller skate and being patronised by the lesser of the ambulatory, my life is jammy. Sometimes, it feels too comfortable, and I fight the nagging anxiety that my luck will run out. Occasionally the fight is against the urge to give it a push and tip everything over into disaster. No one ever mentions the best part of when it all goes wrong. As the sky finally falls, you look up with relief and smugly think, I knew this would happen. Worry is often worse than reality. I married my best friend over two decades ago and we have two happy healthy children. I wouldn't recommend a spinal cord injury or alcoholic parents, but it worked out for me.

When we were in North Carolina, I asked Grandpa, and not completely innocently, if he had any regrets. He replied, Absolutely not. A vehement and unarguable no.

Maybe he is right. What purpose would the hair shirts serve? For the small cost of preserving Grandpa's pride, let him have his exile. A few years after our visit, he would lose an arm to sarcoma; thine offending hand had been stricken from thee. He often recounted stories about his generosity to strangers in need. After his years as a high school guidance counsellor, he boasted of the grown men that called him Dad.

Momo explained, Grandpa was two people. Like all of us, he was the person he was and the person he wanted to be seen as. The cruelty with which he treated my dad was because it was a disappointment that he felt for himself. He never accepted Dad as beyond his control and he resented Dad's success. He was a good grandpa to you and that was enough for me to love him.

Grandpa, for many years, sent long emails, his Sunday sermons he called them. When he was alive, I didn't try to understand what he was communicating. In one of them he wrote, *We have talked about so many things over the past years and said very little*. Then later, *My grandson dug up a purple flower about thirty years ago and gave it to me. I replanted the bulbs next to my new barn and it is blooming right now and as pretty as ever. One day, if he ever moves back to the States, I may give him that little plant so that he can think of me.*

The bulbs came from the River House, where Dad explained chemistry to me with oak leaves. The flower was an amaryllis, a naturalised species, that flourishes in Florida's sandy soil. Giving Grandpa those bulbs was Dad's idea. I remembered the flowers as red and white, but he was correct that, when I see an amaryllis, I think of Grandpa and Dad.

For many years, I kept a cordial distance from my father. After I had recovered from my car accident, I returned to university in Austin, Texas, and Dad came to visit Sarah and me. That trip ended abruptly with me putting him on the first flight back to Florida, determined that Sarah would never have to deal with the frightening disorder that an addict brings with them. I drove him in my wheelchair-adapted van towards the airport on Austin's spine, the I35 highway. Harsh sodium-yellow streetlights spoiled the sunrise's pinks. That van had made my return to university possible. My entire family pitched in to help purchase it, my dad most of all.

I could plead that my father's pain was his alone and I, as his son, was not obligated to take any more than I had already. Surely, our past, his past, makes me blameless, but I do blame myself. In the months following the twins' birth, Dad was different, and I wanted my daughters to have a grandpa like I did. I have only good memories of Grandpa. I don't remember a raised voice, never mind being hit. He was always bragging about his family, his grandson especially. In all our photos together, he is holding me, both of us smiling. My daughters could have a grandpa like that.

One day, if he ever moves back to the States, I may give him
that little plant so that he can think of me.

For years and years, the family talked about *when* we'd move back, except for Momo. She said she had known since I was two, when she saw the future in the backyard of our house in New Mexico. No matter how much she wanted that moment in her life, the joy of being a mom, to remain, it would not. There would be sadnesses and heart-breaks. Momo has told me that she sees my accident, over and over. She stands beside the restaurant where I worked as a waiter. She sees my truck pull into its parking space; the back of my head visible in the back window as I gather my waiter's apron from the passenger seat. On the other side of the parking lot, there is an auto repair shop with a white Camry missing its doors and engine. She sees me pass in front of the truck with its faulty emergency brake. She lies beside me as I die. She smells the oil, the burning flesh, before she bolts up in bed retching. After the dream, she paces the house until the terror subsides.

Sarah returned from Las Vegas with the flu and a story about her coworker getting pneumonia and being hospitalised. The world unfurled mothballed stupidities, but we once again lived cocooned and unaware. That year of travelling with newborns had taught us how small we could live. We had removed ourselves from the churn of anxiety and anger everyone else was feeling. With the lockdowns and job furloughs, we folded away our everyday life and returned to just us and the girls. Sarah didn't have to commute. We took turns parenting, cooking and working. Instead of wandering Mediterranean hills and Mexican beaches, we became tourists in our own London. In our hour of exercise, we discovered a handful of churchyards and tucked away green spaces that we had ignored in the decade living in this neighbourhood.

My anxiety about what kind of dad I was had gone. I no longer wondered if I was a good man because there are no good men, nor bad either. I am to my family an accumulation of moments. The balance, so far, favours me. Mostly it was because the girls grew a little older and were easier to manage. A toddler can be inconsolably miserable, never mind having two of the goofballs, but I get it. Their lives are filled with *can't*. Disability hands you *can't* by the bucket. I'd love to throw a toy at someone's face the next time I am told I can't. Toddlers can't say what they need to say, can't go where they want to go. They are dependent on knuckleheads. When they get what they desire, like sticking a power cord or a dead wasp in their mouth, their angry shouty Papa takes it away.

At the time, Maude was referring to herself in the third person, which was adorable, and to me by my first name, which I found annoying.

I was reading a book, and she took advantage of my distraction to take my wheelchair for a joyride around the flat. I heard her bumping along the walls and giggling. Maude got it, she said, before I offered help. She was already well rehearsed for my over-concern. Maude drives Jarred's chair, she said.

Here comes Maude, she announced, Maude is fast. She went across the room and banged into the box that Zed was reading in. Maude giggled and said, Maude is back. She navigated the living room, navigating around the obstacles of us.

The girls were four. The fat on their thighs, my chuletas, had been used up to stretch out their limbs. The babies that everyone thought boys were clearly little girls. I struggled to order the many persons my daughters have been and will be: the newborns with rattling cries that hurt your heart, the six-month-olds with duelling looks of bewilderment and easy-come smiles, the fists full of 'no!' toddlers, and these little girls about whom I could confidently tell the babysitter: if there's anything I've missed, ask them. They were growing too fast. Every parent warned us, and we were still unprepared for the velocity. I wanted to linger among their past selves, to revisit, to understand the permutations so that I made the best use of the brief time I had with the next Zed and Maude I met. They goaded the pace of the leaps forward. I was, am, will always be a fixed point. A promontory by which they calculate their speed of travel.

That pause in our lives aggravated the leaps in time. The human body and mind are not equipped for the constant seesaw back-and-forth to-and-fro you feel as your children grow up.

Near our flat was St Matthew's churchyard. It was a respite from the onslaught of the city's right angles. The eighteenth-century stone walls are irregular, patched with maidenhair ferns, dandelions and the small purple flowers of self-heals. Here the girls could range without me worrying about traffic or kidnappings. It will be where the twins learn to ride a pedal bike while drunken 'family groups' on benches with takeaway spritzes cheer them on.

It was a gorgeous London summer day. I have grown fond of the seasons here. I endure the dark, grey winters because without them there is no spring to look forward to. My childhood in Florida was without seasons and the difference in the length of day throughout the year is barely noticeable. Time was harder to measure there.

Maude was sitting near the trunk of one of the ancient plane trees that guarded the perimeter of the churchyard. Her full attention was on building a fairy fort. I'd pushed through the thick grass and arrived with a lap full of twigs and branches for her construction. She looked up at me, held a leaf aloft for a moment and then let it drop. We watched its graceful leafish descent. She beamed. I nodded and we watched her do it a few more times.

Zed called me over to show me what she was playing with. A snail was making its way across the lip of a stump. She pointed at the undulations of its wet green leathery foot. Zed turned her body towards me, hands on my wheelchair, but her eyes were transfixed. She whimpered and buried her face against my lap, but her gaze returned to the slow tap of its lower tentacles. I said, don't be afraid, and demonstrated by touching its eye stalk. The creature paused its explorations, and the black spot of its eye pulled into its body before extending again. She put her hand out, finger extended but turned away. Then, she did it. She poked a snail in the eye.

She chittered, I am a big girl, I am brave. Maude walked up to us and without hesitation jabbed the poor creature's eyes.

The girls were meant to start reception in September, but lockdowns made that uncertain. Primary school years had been a recurring topic for Zed. As the snail made its deliberate but ponderous escape from our poking, she asked what year you are in when you are eight. The twang of cockney in her accent made me smile. Having not grown up in England, I did the mental conversion from American elementary grades to British primary years.

You'll be in year three or four, I told her.

She picked up a stick to thwack the stump and declared, I am eleven.

At that age, you are in secondary school.

She was impressed by this information.

What it is like being eleven? I asked.

For her, eleven meant she walks to school on her own and climbs trees.

You climb trees now, I suggested.

Eleven-year-olds climb trees really high.

Okay, I said.

She wandered off, pretending to be an eleven-year-old. Maude followed behind, hands behind her back, a miniature umarell to Zed's diligent stick-based sounding of an old fox hole. London was quiet without its cars and people. Quiet except for the air ambulances that rushed towards the Royal London Hospital. Some days above our idyll there was a queue of red helicopters circling. A man in his home office looked down at us, watching the girls and smiling.

Zed turned her head and ran back towards me in that funny stiff-arm way that children run. It was as if a transparency was brought down over the scene. I see her as a four-year-old overlaid with the young woman she will be. I recall memories of her teenage years that I have yet to experience. Twenty, thirty years are crossed and there is anxiety over an issue she was having, will have, might have. She has a decision to make. The kind of decision that only a young woman must make, and she has turned to me, her father, for advice. Her eyes are wet, and her neck has gone blotchy red from worry. She sits on a sea wall on a beach in a place where I have yet to live. I smell the sea and the pepper of pines from my Floridian childhood. The familiar whiff of marine diesel is there too, and I wonder what circumstances would have precipitated me ever moving back to Florida. But I don't recognise this beach. The sea is clear and still like the Gulf of Mexico, but the water is more topaz than the turquoise I remember. Beyond my adult daughter is a bright clear day and a hill mottled with dark pines and buildings of dusty pink. There are no hills in Florida.

Zed is talking and I strain to hear her from decades in the past. I'm keen to suggest options without prescribing solutions, aware that I only know a fraction of this young woman's life. A couple walking past us are speaking French, trying not to look at Zed, who is upset, and the old man beside her. Have we moved to France? Zed has shed my definitions of her, but our relationship feels intact there in the future, and it fills me with relief. A thought comes to me: we are in Marseille. There is the striped shadow of the calanques bowing towards the Mediterranean. The large tower blocks are pitiable beneath that banded architecture aeons in its construction. Then it is over.

Maude was at my lap, looking into my face. I panicked looking for Zed. Zed was still at the fox hole.

Papa? Maude said and put her head in my lap. I petted her hair. The girls never noticed these jumps in time. I felt fear and regret that I might not see this future. Statistics say that because of my disability I have less than twenty years with them left.

After the fox hole had been sufficiently plumbed, Zed asked if I had a snack.

Maude wanted mango. Jarred, do you have mango?

Call me Papa. Everyone else calls me Jarred, only you and your sister call me Papa.

As we walked back to the flat, I thought about that beach I saw with adult Zed and what it would be like to move again. We both worked from home. The deadline of Brexit was approaching. Soon our red passports would be meaningless, stripped of our 'right to abode'. The girls were small enough, not quite beholden to English as their only mother tongue. Maybe by moving to France, we could stuff full our Now with the newness, confusion, excitement, and stress of living in a foreign country again. Maybe with my head occupied with formulating sentences such as 'Où est l'aire de jeux?' my daughters would be less likely to slip away into the future. Maybe twenty years is enough while I watch the sea, the oldest of Earth's gods, rumble and hiss while my daughters play in its foam.

We passed a row of terraced houses. The first had rose bushes. I gently bent the stems for the girls to take turns to sniff the blooms. The second house had a single and enormous lavender full of a variety of bees. We listened to the hum while the flower spikes nodded and bounced as the fat, fuzzy bees landed. Maude wanted to hear the stories of our time in France among the lavenders during our year of travelling.

Did you like France? I asked her.

At the third and final house, a common poppy had exploded from a crack where the pavement met a wall of yellow London stock brick. The girls pulled off the red paper petals. I wished they wouldn't. Poppy blooms are already too brief, but I say 'no' too much, so I let them. I took a pod and dissected it for them to examine the seeds. Without looking up, Zed asked for a story.

Maude, Zed's hype man, repeated, Jarred, tell a story.

I tell lots of stories. I have told them that Queen Elizabeth was a twenty-foot giant, which is why she needed a house as big as Buckingham Palace. For now, I prefer my girls to live in a world where a giant had a house that was appropriate for her size, rather than a normal-sized woman benefiting from her uncle's taste for American rough.

Tell us about when we were tiny tiny babies.

I have made myths of their births. Maude was born with a pig's tail, and we have the dried remanent, her umbilical cord, as proof. I told them the story of being impossibly small babies. They have heard the story of when they were tiny babies countless times. It was a favourite of theirs and a favourite of mine. After my flip into the future in the churchyard, I was pleased to return to the stable assurance of the past. I told them once again. When they were born, Zed through the door, Maude through the transom. They were the tiniest of tiny babies. So small that we booked a plane trip to a faraway land called Mexico and we didn't even have to buy tickets for them. They rode in my shirt pockets. When we landed, we waved at all the people smiling at the incredibly tiny, bald babies. At night, they slept beside us on the beach, each daughter in one half of a coquina shell. They had a fluff of coconut fibre for a pillow and the corners of a tortilla for a blanket. For fun, they rode on the backs of minnows in the Río Cuale.

After scattering the commas of poppy seed to sow more flowers among the cracks, Zed led us home. The charcoal smudge of the calanques was cutting the horizon above our flat. Tangles of jasmine vines have swallowed the wall around our patio garden. That scent will always remind me of that home. We planted them when we moved in a decade ago, the longest we have lived anywhere.

Those cliffs I saw were not above the East London of our Now. They could stand above us somewhere and some day in the future. I was raised in the brutal flatness of Florida, where every year hurricanes come to scrub the peninsula clean of human error. As a child I made blood sacrifices to the ancient cypress swamps, my offering carried by grey clouds of mosquitoes. If I were to believe in God, it would be of the Old Testament, all caprice and smite. In this France I have seen, we have a benign permanence high above, watching over our family. We could go there, give Sarah and me more horizon to be a couple. Give my daughters hills and mountains to add to the drawings of our family. Give them a beach to play on, let them know the marvels I knew growing up by the sea, but without its dangers. Wet sand between their toes, the taste of salt waves and flocks of seagulls like ticker tape above our picnics.

When we first moved to Marseille, we rented an apartment across from the beach for six months. I saw the topaz sea, pink hills and the pines where future Zed will meet that old man she knows as Papa. Both of my girls will have to reconcile him with the omnipotent, omniscient father that they once confused me for. How could they not? With a kiss, I took away their pains. There was no jar that I could not open. Momo had taught me, and I taught them how to keep away bad dreams by sleeping with your head at the foot of the bed so nightmares can't find you.

When the girls look back and see that the magic that I used to open the parking gate was a remote in my pocket, that manhole covers are just manhole covers and not from where street-cleaning monkeys emerge at night to sweep up the goober eggs (my name for used nitrous canisters East London was awash in), I hope that, though I may have disappointed them, I have never failed them.

Momo tells me she has kept a letter she wrote to her mom when I was a baby. Her mom had laminated it and, after she died, Momo kept it. She had written to my grandmother after I had had a bad reaction to my first vaccinations. My right leg had swollen to twice its size. My skin had gone shiny and red. Momo stayed up all night with me and wrote to her mother about how she understood now what my grandmother had done for her. Momo saw her mother's misery and that she didn't have the strength to fight her demons. In that letter, Momo forgave her mom.

After a swim in the sea beneath an insistent November sun, I was sure we were not moving back to London. I had started to collect the rags of memories to write this book. Sarah was working from home during that brief period when companies forgot that half the fun of having serfs was to watch them toil below your castle tower. We took breaks for tea and chatted on the balcony. Each evening, the four of us made dinner together as the apartment was filled with Fauvist winter light, and the shadows of a starling murmuration drew living shapes on our balcony.

Without having to commute across London, Sarah had time to go running. The apartment had enough space for her to set up a sewing machine, something she hadn't been able to do since we have been together. We found a school to take the girls in the new year. Until then, I took them to Parc Borély while Sarah worked.

A boy approached the girls while they played on the merry-go-round. When he spoke to them in French, they ran away. Maude asked if I brought toys. Zed whined about me not bringing toys.

I said, Don't hit me with them negative waves so early in the morning.

Zed dug around in my wheelchair bag looking for the toys she didn't bring.

I remember where you bought this bag, she said. She gave me directions for the shop starting from an ice cream place in London we used to frequent.

She said, I prefer London.

To Marseille?

She told me she had a good school and good friends. She liked her apartment.

I know it was grey all the time, but I didn't mind, she said. The line about the grey came from my practised answer when a local asked in French why we moved from London. The pang of the accusation hit, and I wanted to defend our choice to move. But I couldn't and I shouldn't. Four-year-olds, soon to be five, have opinions too.

Maude said, I have to go pee.

We found some bushes, Zed following us, but Maude was unsure about squatting. I told her, Did you know that if you pee on a tree, it is yours until someone else pees on it? Dogs made that rule. I mimed a technique learned from a friend in Texas. Despite my lack of labia and that I was unable to stand to demonstrate the slight bend in the knee and forward position of the pelvis, Maude mastered it on the first attempt. Seeing her sister's success, suddenly Zed had to go and claimed a tree for herself. Years later they still point out all the trees that are theirs.

On the first day of school in France, Zed rode her bike and led the way. She kept saying, We have to get there. She has already imbibed my anxiety for being late. Maude rode in my lap even though she was too big.

We're twenty minutes early. Do you guys want to sit somewhere?

I want to wait at the gate, Zed said. Zed kept her bright pink helmet on. It had a blue jay feather from Florida and an iridescent mockingbird feather found in London sticking out the top. I had told her they had good juju and made her go faster. There was also a 'Bollocks to Brexit' sticker, a ward against mendacity. When the school opened, my daughters were the first inside among the flutter of small shoes, red-faced lamentations and mother fuss. They did not wait for me. Zed put her coat on her peg, found her name card and stuck it on the attendance wall as she had been shown at their orientation the week before. Maude sat on a mat looking around her. I left dazed, surprisingly hurt by their lack of need for me.

One of the reasons we moved to France when we did was because the girls were at the right age to have another mother tongue. Over the few years we've been here, my French has improved, and it is a marvel to understand clearly what had been an impossible jumble a month ago. I no longer say, 'Good sausage' when I mean 'Happy New Year'. It only took a year for my daughters to fluently tell little boys they couldn't play on the merry-go-round with them. When they play together, they bounce between the two languages. When Zed gets excited about something, it is inevitably expressed in French. For that reason, I often think her French is spoken louder than her English.

The other day, as I took them to school, we stopped for breakfast at the bakery. The girls ordered for themselves as I found us a table outside. I watched Zed in her mismatched clothes, shirt as always on backwards, as she pointed me out to the baker. She must be ordering me a coffee. Maude came to me a little timid.

How do you say muffin? she asked.

I told her it was muffin but in a French accent.

As we ate, I told them how amazing it was to watch them speak French.

Zed said she remembered the first time she ordered a baguette by herself. She stood to do what we often do, tell a story about our lives together. Not an explicit lesson but one she has learned: to save these treasures because it is what we treasure. She performed the unwrapping ceremony like we've shown her.

She performed the scene while Maude and I watched.

Deux baguettes, s'il vous plaît. Merci. Au revoir.

I asked if she remembered the bakery.

Yes, the long one by the beach.

Where we used to live, Maude piped in.

That's right.

Maude marched into the bakery and asked for a little sack to save her muffin for later. These little girls are so confident. Unafraid to speak to adults. They have been so easy to raise.

Zed asked me if I knew any American folk songs. Her school had students from all over the world and they wanted the children to showcase a song from where they are from.

What about Lead Belly? I said.

Maude suggested the diarrhoea song. If you're hanging upside down and your face turns brown, we sang.

While Maude and I laughed, Zed said, Not appropriate.

As we passed a fountain, we were talking about Maude needing a bus pass.

I need a new photo. Not a baby photo.

That's right. We can't have a photo of Maude like this, I said, and demonstrated Maude's first passport photo with her little turtle mouth and big wide eyes. It's another one of our stories. Maude didn't open her eyes for her first week or so. The first time she did was when we were getting her first passport photo. She looked like the Ko-omote, the chubby-cheeked woman Noh mask.

She had big cheeks, Zed corrected. I blew out my cheeks to perfect the expression.

Do Zed's baby passport, Maude chimed. Zed was generally a mellow baby until her photo was taken. Her photo is recreated by pulling my head into my shoulders and making an exaggerated crying face.

Remember when that was ice and I stepped on it, Maude said, pointing at the fountain.

You can't step on it now, Zed said.

That's right, I said and explained atoms as the Lego of the universe. I talked about water being two hydrogen Lego and one oxygen Lego. I told them that when water was liquid it bounced around, but as it became colder, the atoms had less energy, they couldn't bounce as much so they got more and more stuck together. That was why Maude could walk on ice but not water. The opposite was true as well. When they get hot enough, they bounce like crazy and boom, they bounce right out of water and they become vapour in the air.

Maude cupped her hands and said, I've got atoms in my hands.

I peered into her cupped hands.

You have millions of atoms in your hands.

They were both astounded by this.

Zed wanted to know if they were dangerous.

No, it's air. There are nitrogen and oxygen atoms. There is water vapour there. Remember the hydrogen and oxygen when you stick them together. Dust and pollen are made up of different atoms like carbon.

I learned something new, Zed said.

And we're not even at school yet, Maude said.

The house is built on the side of a hill. The entrance is on the top floor with most of the house below, but I don't go inside. The grey asphalt shingles and ageing clapboard siding resemble a tattered American flag. I pull myself onto the roof and sit on the ridge. I'm momentarily confused as I watch Buddy Hackett gurning his way through *It's a Mad, Mad, Mad, Mad World*, Stanley Kramer's slapstick anti-consumerist film that grossed 60 million dollars. Behind the screen is a Googie-style 1950s futuristic ziggurat with a sign that reads 'Starlight Drive-In Theater'. I understand that I am seeing the home of the dead. The honey-sweet smell of cornfields just before harvest brings with it a sense of regret as my grandpa sits beside me. We watch the field between the house and the drive-in pulsate with fireflies. It is a sea of yellow-green light undulating and swaying in the darkness. My attention is directed to the utility pole beside the house with its web of electric wires. The pole vibrates with malevolence. As soon as I reach out to touch it, I wake.

The rumble surged and fell at the kettle's click. The girls were crowding me as children do. I should have cautioned them, but parenting is marked by these lapses, more easily recalled than any of its successes. A jostle. A bump. A splash of boiling water. I was glad it was my lap and not a child's head.

As a paraplegic, it is easy to damage yourself without noticing. Once, I was in bed to take my shoes off and a sluice of blood followed, thick as cherry jam, onto the sheets. Blood had soaked through my sock unnoticed. I couldn't know when or how I had hurt myself. It was a ragged cut on the back of my heel that eventually had sealed itself with a black clot.

The irony is that I have pain most of the time. The girls are used to their father's unexpected winces from unprovoked neuropathic pains.

'What's wrong, Papa, crazy pain?' one of the twins will say, and kiss my knee to make it better.

After I had burned myself with the kettle, I peeled the wet trousers away from my skin. There wasn't much of an ache, but I knew it was best to check as the girls stood at the bedside asking questions. The burn was a bad one. I still have the scar there in the shape of New Zealand.

Can you go get some ice for me? I asked.

They elicited help from their mom, excited to have a task. After I'd had some pain medication and an ice pack, Maude came into our room, kissed my knee and sat on Sarah's side of the bed. She arranged her markers in a semicircle around herself. The afternoon light was coming through the lowered shutters as she, sitting cross-legged, drew herself flying above houses with triangle rooftops and sash-bar windows despite us never living in a house nor a city that has those types of windows. In her drawing, she has extremely long hair that trails to the ground. I rubbed her back and thanked her for keeping me company.

Often, when I'm working at the dining room table, one or both girls will stand beside me, leaning their bodies into mine. It's a subtle pressure and I keep at whatever I am doing until I find myself at a forty-five-degree angle typing with one elbow pressed against my side. Other times the girls throw themselves into the ever-present lap of a wheelchair dad. I pat their back or rub their heads. Maude will kiss my knee and tell me she loves me, and I am the best. Our affection comes naturally. If Sarah is in reach, inevitably I touch her to check that my luck is real.

On three occasions, my mother-in-law was one, women have approached me to tell me that their father never hugged them. I was never close to my dad like that, they said. My response, each time, always felt a failure. No words could lift the weight of a past never realised. A simple longing never satisfied. An absence made heavy by its presence. Each time I carried their sadness for days.

I had dreamed of my soon-to-be parents waking up to the ochre shades of the New Mexican desert hidden under fresh snowfall. The world was muted to black and white. That morning Momo woke up knowing that she was pregnant. Immediately upon waking I wanted to tell Sarah about the dream, but she was away for work in Rome.

I kept checking my phone for when Momo's status switched to active. As soon as the red circle turned green, I phoned to ask her about this dream. She said, Yes, the day she knew she was pregnant with me was the first time she saw snow.

I asked, Was it a premonition?

She laughed. No. The night before I was lazy, and we didn't take any precautions. Sure as shoot when I missed my next period, I went to the doctor. I knew.

You were wearing a coat that went to your ankles.

It was beige suede with embroidered flowers and fur trim. I loved that coat but when we moved back to Florida, I never had the chance to wear it again.

I asked if she remembers wearing a brown beanie.

You know me. Everything's got to match, even my underwear.

I told her I saw her shuffling through the snow making tracks, catching the flakes on her tongue.

Oh yeah, we played like kids.

You were kids, I remarked.

Before we went back inside, I made snowballs and put them in the freezer to save. Your dad said, you don't have to do that. It'll snow again.

I picked the girls up from school. Maude ran to me, holding a handmade cloud before her like a lantern. Dangling below the cotton ball nimbus were cords of blue construction paper. It was a beautiful object. Kids make you all kinds of uninteresting crap ad nauseum. Dry pasta necklaces that even they won't wear. Slapdash doodles on scraps of paper. Sticky-taped egg carton nonsense that doesn't even look like a bear at all. Not at all. During their month-long fanaticism for origami, if I needed to print anything I had to first eviscerate a paper kitty or whale.

This was worth some Blu Tack, I said to Maude. The highest honour a father can bestow on his young progeny's creations. I suggested she tack it to the wall beside my desk where the rest of the good art goes.

Between my exaltations for Maude's creation, Zed grubbed for praise for a love mandala she had made.

I'm afraid not. Six out of ten at best. Better luck next time, kid.

A young man stopped us. He had a fifth of something nearly gone and he disappeared the last slosh of golden brown before throwing the bottle into the street behind him. He excitedly asked if the girls were my daughters.

He was talking too fast. At the time, my French was okay. A B1 level with oak clusters if I had had my coffee. He poked one of the cherries I was holding, called it a strawberry and laughed at his mistake. As his French flew past, I caught streaks of New World Spanish. He had a tattoo of an AK47 on his arm. I think he said his dad was dead. He wasn't a threat, but I tried to move us along. The girls stared. After we crossed the street, I asked Zed what he had said, and she told me that he was saying that I should be proud of being a good dad.

Less than an hour later, I'm yelling at Zed. As I was yelling, I realised I wasn't angry. Frustrated, yes. It was their dance class that they should be getting ready for. It was grotesque to shout but she was yelling back which threw wood chips on the ugliness burning in me. I went to my room to reclaim my self-possession and sat with the disgust I felt for myself. When I came out, Zed was ready, but Maude was not. Fine, we're leaving without you. She burst into tears saying she couldn't find her shoes.

Okay, let's look for them. They were there in the shoe cupboard. She hadn't looked for them. I threw them into the hall and shouted we're leaving.

Later that night, we were on the couch together and Maude told me, You shouldn't push me when you are mad, Papa.

This afternoon was not one of my best performances, but I hadn't pushed her. We had walked to the dance class with her ten paces behind us crying the entire time. All I had to do to fix the situation was to stop and hug her and that would have been enough. That was it. I understood the mechanisms of Maude. It might not work for ever but that day it would have been the solution. But I hadn't, and, in that little moment, a tiny moment, I was not a good dad. I could have pulled out the splinter that I had introduced but I didn't.

I'm sorry, Maude. I shouldn't have yelled at you.

She continued, At school, the teacher says you shouldn't push me even if you are mad because I could fall and hit my head.

Okay, I said. I still felt guilty though. I have pushed her. Moments where she refused to move, and I pushed her. She was right so I told her that she was right. I should never push. I repeated my apologies.

I am back on the roof of the home of the dead. The firefly sea flickers like the crests of waves at night. No movie is playing. The screen is a grey shadow in the distance. My attention is pulled to the utility pole vibrating malice and danger. Drawn closer, I see there is a seam in the aged wood, and it grows bright yellow teeth, one by one. As soon as I realise they are the heads of yellowjacket wasps, angered by my presence, I wake.

I was still awake at two in the morning, when the phone rang, and Sarah's voice told me from Rome that her sister had sent a message that her mother was in the hospital. Sarah had called to work out the flights. We did that together. She hung up. She called again. Her voice was panicked and confused. This was not like her. She needed my credit card. Hers wasn't working. She was worried about clean clothes. I assured her America still had underwear for purchase. Instead of coming home to Marscille, she was going to be in Florida in twenty-four hours; she would call when she got to her sister's house.

I woke up with the confusing possibility that I had dreamed the phone calls. I didn't tell the girls that Mom wasn't coming home as planned. Fortunately, our school run routine filled the morning, and the topic didn't come up. At the breakfast table, Zed wanted to know why they killed that guy on the wood. I took a long draw on my coffee to prepare myself for the conversation. I figured out she was talking about Jesus. I told her about the Roman practice of crucifixion. The sponge. The spear. The Pietà. The tomb. I talked about the Christian belief in the resurrection. She said her teacher didn't believe in God.

I called Sarah after I dropped them off. She had slept poorly and had been messaging her sisters who live at opposite ends of the US. An Italian TV show chattered in the background. Her voice was flat as we talked logistics.

She said, Tomorrow the girls have swimming lessons. You need to cancel before 3pm so we don't have to pay.

Okay, I said.

I had to cancel the lesson because the pool was not wheelchair accessible. Every week I heard about what they learned and how great Victor the teacher was. Sarah focused on the ever-changing patterns on his Funky Trunks swimwear, a little too much, to be honest. When I picked them up from school, I told them the news about their mom and the swimming lessons.

That's okay, they said. We're going on holiday soon. The apartment has a pool. We can go swimming there.

We had planned upon Sarah's return to revisit the Provençal countryside that we fell in love with after the birth of the girls. For a guy with wheels, I have a perverse attraction to villages built into cliff faces or on the top of fortified hills like Forcalquier or the gorgeous Moustiers-Sainte-Marie.

One of my favourites is the village of Mées. Pillars of puddingstone, a geological oddity made of stones smoothed by million-year-old rivers, jut hundreds of metres above green hills. If you believe the local legend, they are monks turned to stone by a prudish Saint Donat as a punishment for looking under the skirts of captured Saracen ladies. I have been to these places because Sarah was behind me, babies strapped to her chest, helping me to push up the cobbled, steep streets so I could marvel at beautiful medieval buildings glowing pink in the setting sun.

I wasn't sure how I'd manage the girls, our luggage, and the inconsistent definitions of wheelchair access in France. I immediately cancelled the rental car because the rental car didn't have hand controls. I made a few panicked phone calls to friends in London who might be able to take the train down to help me, but it was too short notice, and it was a big ask.

You should still go, Sarah told me.

How's your mom doing? I asked.

She told me. It was not good. She said a friend of hers was asking, Will the girls be okay? How is Jarred going to handle two kids by himself? Sarah had said, He's the better mom. It's not true but it made the point.

I told her a funny story about Zed to lighten the mood. She had brought *The Rainbow Goblins* to school. It's the story of seven rainbow-stealing goblins and how they are drowned by the world's flowers vomiting oily thick slicks of colour. In the final two-page spread, most of the goblins have already succumbed. The green goblin floats face down among the swirl of his robes. The red one, the leader, fights against his fate but we know he is doomed. The blue goblin stares directly out from the page to accuse the reader with fear-wide eyes as swirls of colour fill his mouth to choke his screams. I had received a stern email about Zed being forbidden to bring that book ever again as several other children had had nightmares about it. Zed was upset and didn't understand the problem.

We made it to the holiday apartment despite the woman at the train station's disability-assistance office being unreasonably surly about having to provide assistance to the disabled. Our apartment for the week sat beside a river just like that first holiday when our girls were newborn. Instead of apricot orchards, we were surrounded by a summer variety of yellow apples and cherry trees brimming with bright red eyes. The owners had two granddaughters instead of three little boys. If Sarah was with us, we would have driven to a lake or a river to swim. We would have celebrated the Zed and Maudeness of our lives with stories about them. We would have stopped by a roadside fruit stand for a few sacks full, or a goat farm to buy a few discs of cheese. Instead, our explorations were limited to the girls marvelling at the warmth of the eggs collected from the owners' chickens and the thrill when the granddaughters' tiny tortoise peed when they picked it up. We had no choice but to swim in the apartment's pool, the girls tirelessly shouting *regarde* every time they jumped in. Their fingers were shrivelled and bleached at the end of each day.

We would have gone each night to a different

restaurant on a different hilltop. We would have sat in a village square while our daughters played near a fountain under the shade of plane trees. But these were my worries; the girls were content to walk the verge of the road to the village's only restaurant, a mediocre pizzeria. They raced twig-and-leaf boats down the river, and scrumped cherries, still too sour. They munched happily at dismal pizzas, their faces still marked red from wearing swimming googles all day.

As house martins screeched and flitted between the buildings above us, I told Maude and Zed that house martins always made me think of their mom. I pulled up photos of Sarah on my phone. They shuffled through them. After dinner, we went to the playground, and it was nearing ten at night by the time we walked home. Maude happily marched behind us and ran her hand along the tall stalks of grass, their heads bowing with seed. Zed for no reason at all lifted her skirt at a passing car.

Where is your underwear? I asked. She informed me that she had decided to no longer wear any. I argued the point. She asked repeatedly, But why? while Maude mimicked her sister and mooned me and traffic.

I am on the verge of a country road in France and my daughters are mooning the headlights of passing cars late at night. Our laughter is loud and bright in the canopy of cherry trees.

Sarah, elsewhere, sits beside her mom whose lips and fingers have gone blue. The spirit is gone but the heart is a stubborn organ. It beats and beats and beats because it doesn't know what else to do. Doctors tell Sarah, her sisters and her mom that several cancers have rooted throughout her body. The doctors predict two months, maybe. Her mom closes her eyes and tries to get her heart to see reason.

There was a young couple on the train back to Marseille. The girl was curled against the boy like a Pietà, her legs thrown across his lap. He put her arms around him, and she nuzzled his neck before falling asleep. Watching them I was overwhelmed with the need for Sarah's touch.

The girls knew that Grandma Jane was sick. And that was it. I hadn't said dying. The only thing that my daughters knew was they missed their mother. I hadn't told them that she wasn't likely to come back for several weeks.

Maude said, I want Mummy.

I said, Me too.

Zed said, It's not your fault.

The story I was waiting to tell was that their grandma Jane was dead. Somehow, dying is scarier than being dead.

Sarah was away for a month. The day she was due to be home, Maude asked if Grandma Jane was okay.

No, she died. That's why Mommy is coming home today.

Maude asked if that meant we wouldn't talk to her on the weekend anymore.

That's right.

Zed said she was sad.

Dad had heard Sarah's mom was ill from our intertwined family grapevines, but none of the details. He told me a friend of his from the Air Force didn't have much longer either. I thought I heard his voice choke up. He switched the topic and reminded me of an interview I did. He told me I had said my first book changed our relationship. He said that's not true. That it was when the girls were born.

I said, Thank you. He has been a wonderful grandpa. I talked about how he video-called the girls, his 'zoom school' when he would entertain them with songs, stories, magic tricks and games, his arms appearing and disappearing from the pixelated fog of a 1950s cover of *The Ugly Duckling* that he used as his background. We hung up shortly after but not before he said, You should call Momo.

Despite our relationship having started by phone, Sarah and I were surprisingly bad at it while she was in Florida caring for her mom. When she returned, after the girls went to bed, we laid together, chirping and cooing like two birds mated for life. I teased her about being disappointed that I hadn't moved any furniture. It's something she does every time I travel for work, to the point that the girls make a joke of it too. We talked about flying back for the memorial.

Sarah's grief drowned her every time she opened her mouth. It poured in, all the times she could have visited, called, done that which she didn't.

It is always never enough, I said, over and over. I coaxed her to talk about her mom. We laughed about how she never got the video calls right, so often we would be talking to a pair of eyebrows. Eyebrows that Maude wields with the same expressive dexterity. How through the week, she made bullet points of the things she wanted to talk about with Sarah. A catalogue of mundane victories and setbacks: squabbles with other family members, an old friend emailing, lunch with the family member once the squabble was over, DIY plans and her favourite sport of baiting telemarketers. When Sarah and her sisters were around her deathbed, a telemarketer called and her mom answered it, knowing it was a telemarketer, and quipped, Sorry I'm too busy dying of stage four cancer. Don't call me.

I woke up the next day and took care of the girls to let Sarah sleep. She rose for a lunch of cheese and bread then fell asleep on the couch. She blamed the jet lag but the ghost of her mom beside her told me the truth. Her work had given her time off. She stayed in the house, wearing her mom's clothes and earrings. While I was working if our shared music account switched to Rod Stewart, her mom's favourite, I knew it was Sarah and I would log out.

The plane circled above Florida before landing. The land is speckled with sinkhole lakes like a thousand antique mirrors.

Florida is not just one of the rainiest states, it is built upon water soluble limestone. Newly born lakes regularly swallow houses and their sleeping occupants. I thought that after the first few times a school and all its children and teachers disappeared into a black circle of impenetrable water, something would have changed. The news used to follow the story for weeks with the images of divers rising above the surface to shake their heads and of the vigils at the banks of the new lake. But nowadays, people expect a few dozen children to be sucked underground each week, and they are still building subdivisions on the weakening soil.

My homesickness is always the most intense in that first blast of tropical heat. I feel my gills opening, I told the girls. I rolled down all the windows of the rental car to let in the light of the setting sun. My favourite time in Florida is at night when flowers are at their most boisterous. The perfume-thick air in call-and-response with the cacophony of frogs, insects and birds. It always takes a day or two to remember that this is no longer my home, and it is this sadness that follows me back to France.

Dad met us at a playground. He pushed the girls on the swings. They had called for me to do it but the mulch on the playground made it impossible with the wheelchair.

A little boy was trying to climb onto the swing occupied by Maude. He was aggressive and Maude was afraid. He ignored my dad's repeated 'no's. When the boy pulled at her leg, Dad delivered him to his mother who was unaware and chatting with a friend on a picnic blanket.

I wouldn't have handled it as well as Dad. I would've become angry. I would have said something to the parent and caused an argument.

He set the boy down and said, Here's your mom. The boy didn't know what to do for a few beats, until he followed Dad and gave him a hug before he sat next to his mom who still hadn't noticed anything. Dad returned to playing with the girls and Maude's award-winning laugh filled the playground again.

Dad took a break, sweating and breathing heavily from the relentlessness of the girls' play, but soon Zed wanted the grandpa monster to chase them again. He popped up immediately. On another of his breaks, I wanted to tell Zed to give Grandpa a rest, but it wasn't that Dad needed it. It was me, I wanted my dad's attention. When they threw themselves into his bear hug, I remembered doing the same when I was their size.

If my becoming a parent hadn't opened the possibility of knowing a different father, my understanding of him would have been fixed by the past. My daughters would have only known him as the boogie man that haunted the stories of my childhood.

In that playground, while grandpa monster chased the girls, I dug a hole. The grey quartz sand of Florida made it easy work. Soon the earth turned black and striped with earthworms. I took out those childhood stories I had been carrying, faded and worn, and put them at the bottom face down, pushing an iron nail through their centre. After the hole was filled, I disguised the spot with leaves lest some other curious child find them.

On that same trip, we visited Momo. She was frighteningly thin when she greeted us in the driveway. She waved away my concerns. After I commented on the blossoming of bruises on her arms from her hyperactive dog, she shushed me. She wanted to help me put together my wheelchair, but I told her the girls had it. Like a racecar support team, they were well drilled at getting my chair made and at my car door for me to transfer over.

During our visit, I had to recalibrate my understanding of her. The narrative she created, the narrative I believed and feared, was that she was always close to death. When my stepdad died, Momo kept saying, he wasn't ever sick, never even a cold. There was no plan for if her husband died first. Even with all the evidence I had, I couldn't shake off the fear that she wouldn't recover from his death, but she did. The story I had was that she was bad at taking care of herself and too occupied with taking care of the men in her life. We are both learning that story was not true either.

Since his death, she has fixated on giving away things. She pulled out huge tubs of beanie babies. The girls picked out a few, suggesting she donated the others. I asked about her health. She talked about her appointments. The medicines they had her on needed a tweak; the headaches were awful, but it seemed to be working. There was also a new medication, but it was expensive and, this being America, she rationed it. She still smoked even after I watched her angrily throwing out the vape kits that killed her husband. I didn't say anything. What would be the point of nagging? I have resigned myself to carrying that guilt when she is gone.

I did this a while ago, she said, holding a notebook. But I wasn't ready to give it to you yet. Now is the time. Before she handed it to me, she flipped to the back. There was a photo of me at two years old. It was the photo of a story that I knew well.

I turned two in July 1978, but, looking at the Polaroid, there were too many dead leaves for summer, and I was in long sleeves. Momo's story is that I was looking out past the low wooden fence into the world beyond our yard. Momo had given me a cookie and I stepped outside to eat it. When I heard her behind me, I turned around and looked at her. It was the moment she knew that I was going to grow up and leave her like all the other men in her life. On the opposite page she has written, *Favorite Jarred stories*. They capture key moments of our relationship: the first half are funny stories from my childhood. She only had to write *Big Raisins, Mommy* for me to know what she meant: she had discovered me in the pantry with an empty box of prunes excitedly declaring, Big raisins, Mommy.

The middle ones are from when our family fell apart

and she was trying to get sober, *Chase you all over the River House.* It was a terrible time, but I understood why these stories were here. It was a point when our relationship could have broken but didn't. These are the moments that make a relationship, more so than the good ones. After those few entries, the stories return to funny anecdotes: *Viking Funeral for a Rodent.* I was a teenager by this time. I had carved a mouse-sized dragon boat in art class for my pet mouse that had died. Booboo's pyre included grave goods such as food pellets and a piece of felt he was fond of. I used the remainder of his litter hay to ensure the pillar of smoke was sufficiently strong to carry him to mouse Valhalla.

We all decided to get ice cream and go to the beach on the island that I grew up on, driving along the endless highways built across the water. A flock of black-hooded green parrots flew in formation beside our car. I mourned the huge white houses, like unwanted teeth, that cut through the mangrove wilderness of my childhood.

I had forgotten that I grew up with everyday miracles of the tropics. It was normal to watch a family of dolphins sporting in leaping arcs as you waited for a traffic light to change. I knew by instinct to pick out manatees from the shadows above submerged sandbars. Momo was amused by me pointing out those ancient demigods as if I had forgotten how commonplace they were. I was thankful that I had, that for a moment I could see them as mythical creatures. I made stories for the girls about how they used to have huge blue eyes and traded them for the useless black button ones that they have now. Their vision exchanged for future sight. They can tell you your future, but they know it does not matter, so silently and slowly they drift. A race of blubbered Cassandras.

We sat on the powdered sugar sand of the beach while the girls and Sarah played in the water. It was the same beach where Sarah and I started our life together. Another everyday wonder arrived in the shape of an anvil-shaped thunderstorm at the horizon while we sat under a perfect sky of full sun. I missed Florida thunderstorms, the rain that chewed at roof tiles and thunder that rattled the windows to remind you of your insignificance and how frail a thing a home is.

On the way back, I told the girls about the time I drove Momo around in the banana-yellow Mustang playing DJ Assault. We laughed and she told her version of the story.

When Momo said she was glad we were almost home, because she had to go to the bathroom, the girls told her how I showed them how to pee standing up. Momo laughed and said she was going to practice the next time she took the dogs out for their walk. If the neighbours complained she'll say it's how they do it in France.

After Momo's husband died, I came back to Florida to help her. I remembered most of all how translucent she became, to the point she struggled to pick up coffee cups. She would stand in the backyard smoking, talking to my stepdad's ghost, and the smoke would filter out of her nearly-not-there body. I also remember those months as the first time in decades that it was just us. We spent our time clearing out the house. For me, I wanted to make space for her. All my stepdad's extra furniture was the first to go. She called us the Gimp and Grannie moving company. With each skip load cleared, the house lightened and rose two inches, making a small gap I had to pop my chair over when I went in and out. I left satisfied that she had room to make this home hers.

When she repainted the house purple, her favourite colour, like the jacarandas that surrounded the house, her opacity returned.

My father is still alive. I don't know how he'll die; that cannot be foreseen. But I know how he will be buried.

The flight back to the United States requires a stopover in London, and we stay with friends in our old neighbourhood. It is hard to move for the memories of the place, still grooved and nicked from our family's passage here. I show the girls the coffee shop with the three steps where I sent them in as toddlers with a contactless card to order their babycinos, and the place we met the junkie nun. We pass the hill that Maude flew down with her fearlessness that I admire as much as I dread. I wasn't there when she fell and took off the side of her face and lost a tooth, but I relive the moment as if I was. Kevin's pub, where the reed of Sarah and I bent but did not break, was newly renovated and unrecognisable, advertising 'Taco Tuesdays'.

Landing in the United States becomes a final unstitching of that first year travelling with the twins, visiting family, celebrating these newest McGinnises. I know I will never come back.

Travelling by car with Sarah and the girls means collecting airsickness bags from all the neighbouring seats on the plane. They are green before we leave the parking lot in an enormous white tugboat of a vehicle. I hand out the bags like hymn sheets; we have some driving to do. The closest town on the map is called Knob Lick. I'm disappointed that the local gas station doesn't have any T-shirts to bring back to our London friends.

A three-hour drive used to be unremarkable, but the years in Europe with reliable public transportation has dulled my tolerance. It doesn't help that the car is full of people breathing into barf bags. The airline's red, white and blue logos expand and contract in the rearview mirror.

The prairie passes, slow green waves slicked with a rainbow of spring flowers. The land was once covered by an ancient oak forest that stretched across hundreds of miles, but generations of immigrants and their steel axes have left only a few trees. Under each dark green canopy, a few head of Black Angus rest.

The highway's shoulder is dotted with cars as people stop to take a photo of themselves among the royal-blue washes of bluebonnets. The firewheels in their multitude look like a coal fire of orange and red. Pink primrose trim the edges of the road beside the yellow-petalled black-eyed Susans. I marvel at this slow silent firework show. I will miss the wildernesses I have known here.

The tradition was to put a pinch of earth in the first son's first solid foods so that he never strayed too far from home and took care of his parents and their land. Since I was born in New Mexico while my father was stationed there in the Air Force, that spell didn't work. Momo had a baby food jar of gypsum, the sediment of a shallow

Cretaceous salt lake, that had been taken from the nearby White Sands national park. She sprinkled a few grains into my apple sauce.

She said, That dirt felt more magical than the stuff lying around our backyard where the cat might have peed.

You ate it without complaint, crunching away, she said. She speculated that using sand from a place where we only lived temporarily had the reverse effect. That I would always crave other lands.

The small homesteader graveyard that we are driving to had been bought by Grandpa's brother to make sure it stayed in the family and was taken care of. It is a small bump of land wrapped by the bend in a creek. It used to be part of a dairy farm and the black iron gates with our family name across it feels a strange formality in this rough-hewn back country.

When we arrive, Sarah stumbles out of the car and is sick against the trunk of the gigantic bald cypress growing in the oldest part of the graveyard. In the South, grave-yards are often built around these trees, which are known to be a gateway between this world and the next. The care-taker tells me later that there has been a graveyard here for five hundred years, long before the first McGinnis was buried. The first graves are marked by homemade bricks of mottled black and red. Most of them have collapsed in on themselves and there are no longer any visible names or dates. In the middle of the cemetery the graves show more craft, and on the granite stone of an aunt I only know from stories, I read, I GO BETWEEN BIRTH AND THE URN A BRIGHT ASH. Another stone is of a mother buried not long after her eighteen-year-old son, William. There are a lot of Williams here. My father was the last one. His grandparents and great-grandparents have their stones here too. They lay in the newest part of this tiny cemetery.

The markers all tilt from the cypress pushing its roots through the soil below. The girls, having recovered from the car ride, head towards a small building with a dented tin roof to throw out their bouquets of filled airsickness bags. The groundskeeper explains later, with pride, that the dent was from a pig being chucked into it during a tornado over fifty years ago. So, the story goes, anyways, he says. All his sentences are punctuated with 'anyways', as if he feels bad for imposing the one or two sentences he speaks.

Sarah still leans against the tree as I watch the shades of the dead rise from their silence. In the daylight, they are hard to see. Like birthday candles at a picnic, they are a flicker-quick glimpse in the shift of the tree's shade. They surround her. They take turns putting themselves where she is, mimicking her posture as the last ripples of sickness subside. They search through their insubstantial forms for the twinges of when their guts heaved like my wife's. The girls move through the graves and read the names of their ancestors. Maude looks at me, crowned by their flicker and says, Poor Mum.

In the distance, the green shoots of what will be autumn's harvest of sorghum pinstripe the tilled black earth. The voices of the dead are easily confused for the static of the nearby creek. They revel in the being of us. Maude's breath. My wife's spit glistening on a stone. The memory of teeth.

The voices of the living are like breezes, they say. They talk about the feel of the caretaker's mower on the grass blades above them. They fondly recall two teenagers in the sixties who used to fuck on their graves. The phrase I hear over and over is, I remember my name.

The caretaker walks and talks with an ambling pace. He is in his seventies, tall and sturdy. He has a cowboy hat with a creased brim and a finely groomed grey beard. He wears jeans with a Masonic square-and-compass belt buckle. A cowboy. When I try to greet him, his wife intercedes and says he's deaf. Her grey hair is cut short. She has a loose white western shirt that moves in the breeze, and a fiddle tucked under her arm; she is as tall and strikingly handsome as her husband. I wait until he turns his head to thank him for organising the funeral. Still not hearing me, he replies that his eye patch is temporary. He is recovering from a head injury.

When the family arrives, we all sit beneath a tent around the grave. No one seems to know what to do. We are a people without ceremony, and it is at these moments that the want of ritual is most keenly felt. I don't have a 'better place' to imagine my dad, only that he is not here. After a discussion about what to play on the fiddle, 'Amazing Grace' is chosen. His ashes are in a black box. They sit on a crate covered by fake green grass and beneath is the freshly dug hole. His father's grave is one over and I wonder how he would have felt about that.

I read a story I wrote for him as a seventieth birthday present. I wrote about him teaching me about atoms and me teaching the girls about atoms forty years later. Each family member gets up and talks about him. The stories are most often about his practical jokes and sense of humour and his constancy. He was always sending emails and phoning family to check in. My younger cousins remember gift certificates appearing in the mail while they were in college and how much they were appreciated. His sisters remember homegrown fruit and vegetables appearing on their porches. His younger sister talks about a house in Alton, Illinois when Dad would pull her up on the roof to watch fireflies and the nearby drive-in theatre. She made a joke about it being why they are all good lip readers. She continues and tells me that he spent a lot of time up there until he was attacked by yellowjackets that had nested in the telephone pole. The meaning of my dream lets loose my grief and the sorrow of others washes through me. Two caterpillars, orange and brown with a line of white dots and two stripes of electric blue, measure the perimeter of the box of ashes. They stretch upward looking for somewhere to go from the box. After the ceremony, I ask the caretaker what kind of caterpillars they are.

They're just bugs to me, he answers. Anyways, he is more interested in knowing, as family, whether I will be buried here too. He shows me a folder he has of the history of the graveyard, with news clippings of the more recent dead, including his son who died nearby because of a drunk driver.

Someone knows enough to take the box of ashes and pass it around. It is a rite, and I am grateful for some act to honour the dead. To recognise this brief moment of consciousness and wonder before our faint glow fades back into another stretch of eternity. I go between birth and the urn, a bright ash.

When it is my turn, I am pleased with the box's surprising heft. We need our father's ashes to be substantial. The weight of fathers must be carried, or you will be buried beneath it. I put my hand on its top, an improvised gesture of reverence. Regrets fall like a surprise afternoon hailstorm. I flinch at every hit. There is a safety latch that saves us from knowing, truly knowing, the death of a parent. Sure, we can pretend to know. We can imagine life without the person, but it is theoretical, a mockup design for the immenseness of the thing itself. As the ashes are passed around. I think about the grandpa my dad became. I wish we had talked more about this. When we visited Florida, he always made no imposition and waited for me to tell him what day he could visit his granddaughters. My steel-girded heart had made a full relationship between us impossible; he had plenty of chances but not quite as many as he needed, Dad with his gardener's patience, showing me time and time again that he could be trusted. When my father read this book, he commented on that last sentence. He wrote, *Between your anger and my shame we were at an impasse, but rather than my patience maybe it was your grace.*

The Last American

This will be the year of their fiftieth wedding anniversary. The car is taking them to their holiday home. There is an orange tabby cat in the back seat named Sais Pas that follows the man around like a familiar.

They have spent the summers there for nearly twenty years to escape Marseille's heat and tourists. Since the twins have fledged, they stay more often and for longer. There is talk about selling the house in Marseille, but the old man in the wheelchair can't imagine giving up the home where the girls spent their teens. There is also the sea to consider. In Marseille, he spends his mornings with the cat at the window to drink his coffee and watch the high tide crawl across the highway and sneak into the ground floor of the abandoned apartments. After his parents died, he never returned to Florida where he grew up, and age has made his memory promiscuous. The scent of the Mediterranean makes do for his childhood remembrances of the Gulf of Mexico. The whiff of sea air conjures his childhood. His memories of his parents are stolen from photos in an old box that he regularly picks through.

The last hour of the trip north into the mountains is their favourite. The old couple share the bread, cheese and an apple butter sandwich Sarah has made, and the old man tops up their teas from a chunky green thermos they have had since they first lived together in the US. Once the car leaves the ferocious speed of the autonomous-car highways, the windows roll down. Awakened by the alpine air, the old couple chatter over scenic viewpoints seen over and over, trees grown or lost, new constructions, and the opening and closing of businesses. The new bakery, probably a year old at this point, is still untried and gets the inevitable round of 'This time we'll go for sure'.

Their village is not even a village. It is a cluster of houses up the hill behind a village that is barely a village. Formally, their not-even-a-village was the estate of Charles Emmanuel II, the seventeenth-century Duke of Savoy, who, despite being more interested in personal pleasures, managed to squeeze in a religious genocide that even Cromwell considered over the top. It's not clear how much time the duke spent there but, in a letter postmarked from the residence, historians have noted the first recorded occurrence of 'snoodling'. He may have even coined the term. Over the centuries the duke's house was chopped up and the surrounding estate parcelled out. There are about fifty houses and apartments. The majority are occupied by retirees like them. They named the cottage 'the House of Love and Squalor' because of its neglected state when they bought it. Mostly though it is referred to as the 'Mountain House'.

In their first year as parents, they circumambulated the hills and mountain towns of France towards the church or castle that lay at the top, Sarah pushing her husband's wheelchair up steep and cobbled streets with two sleeping babies strapped to her. The bumpy landscapes of Europe conjure those uncomplicated feelings of benevolent parenting. They were always the youngest couple getting lost in the zigzag of pink stone terraces clinging precariously to black marl cliffs. That's no longer the case.

Once the car parks itself, Sarah lets the cat out who begins his patrol. She retrieves the wheelchair from the boot.

You be careful, the old man says. He watches his wife, as if his vigilance can keep her from falling. The glass is polka-dotted by her fingerprints as she steadies herself with one hand against the car. When he hears the second wheel click into place, he opens his door and positions his feet to transfer over. She holds the chair as he does. He pulls himself over and adjusts his feet onto the footplates.

Put your seat belt on, she says. Last week, he fell in the shower. Nothing was broken but she had to get the neighbours' adult children to lift him. She kisses his head and goes to get their luggage. He pinches her butt as she passes.

Hands off, you old goat.

The twins, Zed and Maude, will arrive in a few weeks to help celebrate the couple's fiftieth wedding anniversary. The house is too small, but they love bunking together like when they were teenagers. When they are in the house, the old man brings them coffees while they sleep in. He does it because with their sleeping faces they are his little girls again.

Once, Maude peeked open an eye to see the old man staring at her with a bovine grin.

Still sleepful, she asked, What are you doing?

Watching you sleep.

What is wrong with you? Go away. A brief smile and her eyes closed again. He caught that smile and stuck it in his shirt pocket. He shut the door quietly carefully gently and went to tell Sarah what happened. They giggled together and thrilled once more in the joy of their existence.

Those first days back at the cottage, Sarah busies herself opening the house, preparing for the girls' arrival. She orders groceries full of childhood treats that they have abandoned. They bought the mountain house from a time when he used an arts grant to create a line of CBD suppositories laser-etched with lines from famous poems. The process was revolutionary at the time, and the man registered a patent for the automated process for compensating focal intensity for the different molecular weights of polyethylene glycol combinations for the serif type of Simon Armitage's work. It was a financial lifesaver and welcome distraction after the controversy and libel case from his second book.

Maude is in what remains of the United States. Her job sounds important. He brags about it whenever he gets the chance though he doesn't understand what she does. He repeats keywords he has heard her say to Zed. The man complains that her visits are too rare, and constantly schemes with Sarah to precipitate another. Travel isn't difficult, but also, it's not easy. He stays at home more and more. Sarah has gone to see the girls without him several times. Zed is in London. They fret that she doesn't seem happy there, but they try not to pressure her. It is nice to have one of the girls close. Zed will arrive a week before Maude. The car will retrieve her from the station, and they will be waiting in front when she arrives. Sarah will already be crying which will make Zed cry.

The villagers still treat them like their pet foreigners, mascots, thrilled to have somebody from somewhere else appreciate their pine-scented paradise, mostly ignored for the ski slopes north or the beaches south. Though they have been in France longer than anywhere else, being a foreigner suits the old man. As soon as they arrive, the villagers bring baskets filled from gardens or kitchens. Madame Olivier, aptly named, brings a plastic bottle filled with olive oil from her orchard. She writes on the bottles 'organic' with the scare quotes. She calls the man Miami, because he is from Florida, and it is the one city in the state that she had been to. The couple have tried over the years to repay the kindnesses of the villagers, but this only redoubles their efforts. The neighbour's radio drifts into the house. It gives the man an excuse to take a break from his desk. He still writes because it is how he metabolises the bitter salts of a life. He finds Sarah weeding the flower beds to tell her he's going to go visit with Monsieur Passeron.

You two behave, she says, and that is all she says. She's worried that he'll hurt himself again, but she doesn't want him snapping at her for fussing too much.

Sais Pas, stopping to scratch and sniff as they go, leads the old man to his friend's house.

Monsieur Passeron is blind. He spends the temperate days sitting at a small table in the back of his cottage listening to the radio. His English is as serviceable as the old man's French. They flip between the two languages, depending on the topic. The old man has brought slices of bundt cake, a gift from another neighbour. This is excuse enough for Passeron to retrieve his home-made génépi, two glasses balancing on the bottle neck. He dishes the local gossip while Sais Pas sleeps in the man's lap. When the sun sets in the peaks above, they say goodnight and he returns to his wife who is making pasta carbonara.

Maudie is going to want you to make this again.

Sarah smiles. I bought too much bacon, she says.

They go to bed and read before they fall asleep. Her hand rests on his which rests upon her hip bone. It is another ritual well worn into the granite of them.

His first thought in the morning will be cold, selfish and pathetic.

I don't want to die alone, he will think.

He was supposed to die first. He had a six-year statistical disadvantage by gender alone. Paraplegia should have cut away another twenty. Even being left-handed was supposed to cost six months of life expectancy.

The future was supposed to be this. Sarah, the lines at her eyes having made her face more striking, leaning over the rails of a hospital bed whispering, I adore you.

I adore you, he would reply with a voice cracked and desiccated. He would tell her that it will be okay. She will be okay. It's not okay right now but it will be okay again someday. She was going to smile, her eyes shining with tears as he told her she's got the girls to take care of her. That was how this story was supposed to end.

That thought collapses in their still bedroom lit by seams in the window's shutters. He will be shamed by that selfish thought and bury it deep within to pretend it never was. It does not fit the story of her perfect husband.

He will look at her again. She is her but she is not her. The phrase 'looked like they were asleep' comes to mind and he is annoyed by the stupidity of it, its falsity. The truth is that death is understood utterly and sensed easily. Every cell of him glances at what it does not want to admit: this is the only certainty life contains.

This is not Sarah but a corpse. That which made her, that which philosophers and scientists have tried to pin to a board and say this is the person: that is gone. It is not her. A cardboard suitcase, a cheap imitation of what is needed for the journey.

His second thought will be that he didn't like how her mouth was open. She always fell asleep before him. Like a switch, head down and asleep. Travelling long distances, he was always left to fend for himself; she would fall asleep on take-off and wake up at landing. He spent half a century watching her sleep. Her face at rest is fixed as statuary in his mind. The thick clasps of eyelashes. The nose with its bump in the middle. It's a great nose. And her lips thinned in repose. Lips that have been a pleasure for so many years. He closes her jaw so that it matches that carved memory. He will remember her lips as still pink but maybe that isn't true. Her skin having gone pale makes her freckles stand out. One of the first times they lay together, a tangle of limbs, they compared complexions. He was dark from unrelenting Texas summers. She was pale from the Pittsburgh winters. The contrast was satisfying. The decades in the south of France have diminished the difference. This papier-mâché wife is much paler, much older than the real her, which he feels is somewhere still inside if he knew the words to reach her.

He lifts a ribbon of her hair from her shoulder. She

keeps her hair long for him. It suits the shape of her face, he has told her. Running a thumb back and forth across the warp of it, he notices a few threads of gold still shine through the grey. She suits her grey hair, but he liked it when it was brown. When she was younger, she thought brown was boring and dyed it red. He liked it then too. After the twins were born, the grey started to be visible, thread by thread, a new feature, like her widened hips and C-section scar. Signifiers of her new rank.

He talks to her, even if she is not her. He talks to her because they have been talking together for decades. What else can he do?

What are we going to do now? he asks, still with her hair in hand like a silk merchant absent-mindedly appraising quality. The anniversary party is going to be a downer.

You got this kiddo, she says. I miss you already. Come lay down beside me. It's lonely in this big bed. You have to call the girls and let them know.

He lays down beside her. He holds her. Her lips are still soft. Her scent is still hers. It will linger on a pillow after they take the body away. He will try to drown in that pillow's scent until it fades three days later, and he throws it out. He hides his face into the cradle of her neck which has been his refuge.

The bed rocks against the old man's grief. The animal howls make him hoarse; he chokes and coughs until her nightshirt is soaked in tears, snot and spit. Pink brush strokes of blood where he bit his hand too hard make broad sweeps across the sheets. He falls asleep and wakes with a start.

You have to call the girls.

But he doesn't move. He remembers or imagines he remembers that she had made a noise in the night. A shake of the bed. Her reaching out.

If I had woken up, I could have saved you.

You stop that now.

He doesn't listen to her voice in his head. He knits the memory into her having called out his name in the night and gripped his hand until the truth becomes that it was all his fault. He will carry that false regret so heavily that sometimes he will not be able to look his daughters in the eye, which they will mistake for depression.

He straightens her nightshirt, brushes her hair and tidies the loose strands behind her ear. He tucks her in. She loves a made bed. He tells his phone to call Zed but cancels it.

Sarah shouldn't be alone right now. They need to make this call together. He puts his hand beneath the blanket and searches for her. The skin of her hand is soft, but it is not her hand, not her skin. Still, he is careful. He rubs her hand gently. He assiduously avoids her veins. She has a phobia of her veins. Getting her blood drawn always caused panic and queasiness. Her hand is not cold but it's not warm either.

Take a deep breath. Do it again, she tells him as she has told him countless times before.

Another overwhelming sob grows in the pit of himself. He dials the number quickly. He calls Zed, because Maude, six hours behind, is still sleeping.

Hey Pops. How's tricks?

She didn't wake up.

Papa?

Saying it out loud makes it true and he is not ready for it to be true. Zed is talking as he struggles to breathe and golden sparks swim in his vision. It's when he hears Zed's voice rising in panic that he comes back to himself.

Yes, call the ambulance. Yes, I know the number. Okay. Yes, come as soon as you can. Yes, I'll call them immediately. Yes. Yes, see what trains, we'll buy the ticket. I love you too. Yes.

He means to dial the number for the ambulance, but a panic attack overwhelms him. He goes back to his side of the bed and lies down beside Sarah.

Sarah is there in the dream. She says she was looking for him.

Where'd you go? she asks.

I'm sorry, he says.

A knock at the door. Someone is inside the house. He opens his eyes. Madame Olivier is calling 'Miami' through the house. She enters his bedroom followed by a doctor. She tries to coax him into the kitchen.

What if Sarah wakes up and I am not here? All these people are in the house. She won't like that. She is going to be scared.

The doctor is checking her pulse. He looks at the man and looks at Madame Olivier. Another neighbour has arrived, and they help him into his wheelchair. They are older than him and he wants them to stop before they hurt themselves. He struggles to keep down the anger. He lets someone push him to the dining room table. The house is full of villagers. There is a hand on his shoulder. He finds out later that, when he didn't answer the phone, Zed called all the neighbours as well as the emergency number. She woke up Maude too.

Someone has made coffee. Someone else is asking questions. The world comes through a Vaseline smear.

I don't know where my glasses are, he says. Yes, she wanted cremation. What if she's not dead? We have to be sure. Is that right? Did she want cremation? Yes, that's right. He used to tease that he would scatter her ashes in her favourite cheese shops. On the goat cheeses, where no one will notice, she used to reply.

It takes two days before Zed arrives. He hears the car turn on and leave so he knows she has called it from the train. He pulls himself out of bed and realises what bad shape the house is in. Passeron has visited as there is a génépi bottle on his nightstand. He had started putting *really organic* on his homemade liquor as a shared joke between them. He panicked the entire village by thinking the cat was lost. A dozen French retirees were shaking cat treats until Sais Pas was found on the couch in his house. There was an argument with the doctor. He had called the poor man a ghoul for being so eager to get rid of her body. The villagers shepherded him through the administration process. He has been a French citizen for over a decade, but they pleaded for dispensation because he was a foreigner. It worked and the forms were completed and stamped quickly. He remembers breaking his phone against the stone wall when it notified him that social security had sent him 235 euros. That all the infinities she contained could be reduced to such a paltry amount threw him into a fit that brought the neighbours to the house once again. The broken phone only added to his daughters' concerns for him.

The car leaving gives him an hour or so before Zed arrives. He will try to put up a facade of normality. He wants his daughter to mourn her mom undistracted by worries for her foolish father. The throb in his head makes the light on the nightstand pulse menacingly. His mouth is sour. There is a film on his skin and a barnyard stench in his clothes. Each button undone takes effort and the tremble feels like wilful disobedience from his hands. He peels away a shirt stiff with dried sweat. The urge to return to their bed and disappear back to her overwhelms, but putting himself in order before Zed arrives is more important. The thought of her finding him like this is too shameful. In the bathroom, he examines himself. The sag of belly is surprising. He gives the tab of grey flesh a few shakes and marvels at the persistently black line of hair below the navel. He is disgusted by the face of the old man in the mirror. The skin at the jowls and throat hangs indecently. The sallow flesh, the white stubble, is gross.

I am dying, he thinks, as if testing a hypothesis. It is not a displeasing idea. He positions the wheelchair close to the shower, locks the brakes, double-checks that the wheels are indeed secured. He slides himself onto the shower chair, strategically placing his feet before each manoeuvre, testing his weight against the grab bars. He has done this time and time again. His strength is there but he is scared. Once in the shower chair, a bottomless fear seizes him. He can't let go of the grab bars. He feels faint but if he falls no one will save him. No one will hear his shouts. She is gone.

I am alone, he thinks, and that thought is a premise, an axiom, the grounding for everything from now on. Another round of consuming sobs until the scalding shower palliates the ache that has been persistent since they took his wife from him. He uses her fancy soap that smells of marzipan. The last time he smelled it was when he had kissed her wrist. The soap scrapes aways the grime and dullness. He returns to the body he inhabits, broken but serviceable for the days ahead. He dresses in clean clothes and starts to put the house in order before Zed arrives.

The electric whir of the car returning and the timbre of its tires on the gravel path send the man to the front door to await his daughter. He glimpses the car's metallic shine among the thick green curtain of forest. How many times have the girls been retrieved from the station? The old man and his wife treasured that hour of anticipation to chatter about meals to be made, excursions to be taken, and trade concerns about their children.

As the car parks itself, Zed waves furiously, smiling but crying. All the man sees is his wife when she was that age. She rushes to hug her father. She doesn't realise how much her touch pinions him to earth.

I cannot die. There is too much to do. To make them orphans so soon would be cruel.

The daughter crumples into the old man's lap when she leans down to hug him. She sobs into his neck. He doesn't understand what she is saying.

The weight of his daughter is shocking.

Where did my little girl go? My wife is gone. I am losing them all.

The embrace lasts a few seconds, but it feels like he is returning from a long trip the details of which he cannot recall. She touches his face; her hands are still chilled from the car's AC. There's a look in her eyes that is not mourning. She is afraid for her father.

Sarah would be upset that the house is not ready for the girls, although Madame Olivier, despite him yelling at her for cleaning up a tea stain that had been Sarah's, has been coming with her sister to tidy and bring food for him and his cat. The whole village has rendered sympathies big and small these past few days.

It will be a few more days before Maude arrives. Fear makes a talker of Zed, and she does not let silences settle too long in the house. She stands too close, as if she's afraid her father will slip away too. She leans on him, like she did as a child, while watching the birds in the backyard, or when she is reading over his shoulder. He does not mind. Her presence keeps him tethered. Maybe she senses his inclination to follow Sarah. Maybe it is the same for her. The father and daughter don't talk about it, because, when they tried, they fell apart so suddenly and violently that they both ended up hysterically laughing at each other's snot-sodden faces.

He sleeps on his wife's side of the bed or tries to sleep. He feels her absence most keenly at night. Before she died, if he had trouble sleeping or was ruminating some worry, he'd pull Sarah closer, bury himself half under her.

243

Without waking, she would put a hand on him, drawing circles with her nails. That was enough. That is gone.

He listens to his daughter move through the house at night. She watches ancient film noirs, Sarah's favourites. She fusses around the house, constantly tidying. She talks to her sister and others on the phone. She cries alone in her room. He knows what he should do is be the papa who can swallow his daughter's grief, to take this great 'ouchie' from her like his kisses did for a thousand scraped knees and bumped heads. But it doesn't work like that. He and his daughter have struggled to talk about real things. They are too similar. His advice and opinions always annoy her. So, their portions of grief, measured out, must be taken alone.

He keeps forgetting that Sarah is gone. When the truth of it hits, he is overwhelmed again and again. The old man is embarrassed, looks around guiltily, when he returns from reveries hours long where he and his wife have had full conversations. They have discussed the merits of meeting Maude in Marseille when she lands. He tests his suspicions with his wife that something else is bothering Zed. It is the missing laughter that rattles awake her ghost most of all. He makes a joke, but when he glances over to see his wife laughing, he is surprised to find his daughter next to him. He suggests that maybe she might want some of her mom's clothes, pick out pieces for Maude too, and they could donate the rest. When he opens the armoire, the sleeves of his wife's dresses never stop moving, like bunting in the breeze, from the restless motions of Sarah's ghost.

He hears her whispers, but he can't catch the words. Her ghost shakes from the sleeve of her favourite coat as the old man in the wheelchair brings it to his lips. He breathes in the wool's scent. He takes her hand, and the coat pulls him into the armoire. The doors close behind him. He ignores Zed's shouts.

Zed is on the edge of the bed, surrounded by crumpled tissues. She wipes her eyes when the old man emerges.

I can't do it, he says.

You don't have to. There's no rush, she says as she stands. Let's get fondue and wine, lots of wine.

She has a secret to tell you, Sarah says. But she's not ready. She wants to be there for you right now, but she needs her papa. They will never stop needing their papa.

I'm trying. It's hard. I miss you so much.

It's not okay right now but it will be okay again someday. Her ghost smiles; she knows she's being cheeky.

I was supposed to say that.

It's a good line, she says.

Childbirth is a doddle compared to the pain I'm feeling, he says, matching her grin.

I can haunt someone else you know.

For Maude's arrival, they return to Marseille. With their home full of his daughters, in their house by the sea, the ghosts of Sarah are more restful. He sits in the garden next to her empty chair beside a cairn she made over the years from collected stones, shells and driftwood. The washing machine used to rattle and clunk from one of her treasures being forgotten in a pocket. After a shelf broke under the weight of her collection, she started the cairn. The girls have made their contributions to what they call the fairy fort. It has grown taller than the old man in his wheelchair. Even with the cairn, the corners of the house hide demijohns of beach glass, marbles, shells, pebbles, and terrariums that are miniature antediluvian landscapes complete with little dinosaurs added by the girls decades ago. He has always loved the clutter she made of their homes. He teased that her design aesthetic was German granny geologist.

The cairn is mostly local limestone dotted with rocks brought back from holidays: clay reds, pumice blacks and seashell whites stand out like temple votives to successful foreign expeditions. Her baggage was over its weight limit on several occasions, and it is one of the family jokes.

From the house he watches his daughters as they tidy his wife's garden.

Not bad for two goofy kids from Florida, he says.

Go play with your little girls, Sarah says. Stop talking to your dead wife.

They're not little girls any more.

You sure? Look.

Maude has her butt stuck out and Zed smacks it with a broom, at which they explode into exaggerated laughter. Zed does a few strums of air guitar on the broom in time with the ABBA blasting from a portable speaker. His daughters, enchanted by the magic of their home, have reverted to childhood. Their voices are raised; they are giggly. The in-jokes, the teasing, the catchphrases from their adolescence are pulled from attic boxes. The man appreciates the girls keeping him distracted, fed and laughing. The news of his wife's death has spread and, when the family go out to eat, there are awkward messages of condolences, endured and appreciated. At first, he felt embarrassed to bring his grief into restaurants, as if it spoiled the food. But that shames him. Sarah was a love to be mourned openly. He retells the story of finding her dead. He talks about how hard it is without her. How thankful he is for his two daughters who stand around him. People tell him stories about his wife: her kindnesses, her patience, her humour. Each night they come home with comfort food, bottles and more stories. These stories, modulo of him, he retells over and over to his daughters even though they were there when he had heard them.

The crematorium calls. He hands the phone to Maude. After the call, she looks at him. He shakes his head. She takes Zed with her instead.

When Zed and Maude return, they set her ashes on the dining room table. The shape and matte white colour of the urn makes him think of an egg. He tells the girls they chose a good one, but the object stirs up anger. That is not his wife. The temerity of the universe to think his wife can be reduced to a jar of ash. To be put back into an egg to be reborn as someone else's love, no!

Zed says, She can't stay at the house.

What?

French law doesn't allowed remains to be kept in the house. They need you to decide where she'll be interred. We need to register—

No! The sharpness of his voice cuts off the conversation. These women, usually full of confidence, shrink to little girls before their father's shout and defer to his unreasonableness.

He goes into his bedroom, listening to his daughters talking, fretting, discussing, arguing. When the front door opens and closes, he returns to the urn on the table.

You must have been lonely out here? he says. He imagines the ashes packed with a density that makes them unmovable, sinking down to the centre of the earth to become its new core. This is how it should be, but a life barely alights here before it dissolves away. To the universe they are a couple of paltry kilos.

He brings her to see her garden. The girls have done a good job. The avocado tree, first germinated in their kitchen window, is heavy with fruit that are more seed than flesh.

Might even manage two bowls of guacamole this year, he quips. The Zed and Maude trees are robust, an apple and a pear, planted when they first moved in. Every year his wife fretted about the fruit going to waste. Desperately delivering sacks full of it to anyone she could, including tollbooth operators and rest stop cashiers when those were still manned. All the trees are garlanded with either bird feeders or wind chimes.

You left me with enough apple butter to see me to my end, the man says.

A ring-necked parakeet lands on the feeder next to him. She has lost her fear of humans and knows that fat old Sais Pas is not a threat. Sarah had hung the feeder low enough for the man to manage a few pets along the green velvet of her back before she nips at him. She is a messy eater, and two collared doves have landed to peck at what falls from the seed ball.

He takes the parakeet's visitation as a sign of Sarah's continued presence. The neighbours hate these birds as invasive and noisy. An unwelcome reminder of what has changed, like the snow-bare Alps.

He takes the urn to the cairn of stones. He thinks of the decades it has taken to make but how it all happened in an instant, a moment that is now over. The cruelty of that flashes into anger.

Is that it? he asks.

He sets down his wife's remains.

She asks, What are you up to?

He takes apart the topmost tier, setting aside the stones to be replaced. A wind picks up. It strengthens as he creates a niche in the centre in which to pour the ashes. A few rocks tumble away but he ignores them. He feels the wind strengthen but the leaves on the trees are still. The family of carp windsocks they brought back from Japan are undisturbed, but the wind bumps and shoves him. It is loud, he feels the velocity of the Earth itself, the sky disappears, and the stars streak into threads of light. Everything is gone. He feels the tug of centrifugal force and he is about to be thrown into space. The girls will find his empty chair and the half-finished tomb for his wife.

When the girls return from their walk, they find the garden full of Sarah's emptied demijohns.

What have you done? Maude says, as she pulls a sea-polished stone from her pocket. The man hasn't noticed her and is occupied organising glass marbles in his lap.

You've been busy, she says, fear edging into her voice. She puts her hand on his shoulder, and he jerks in surprise. He turns to her, looking at her without comprehension. She examines his face. The lid of his right eye droops. His lips slope to a frown on the right side. Before Maude can react, Zed bursts from the house shouting, Where's Mum?

The doctors said it was a stroke, but not a serious one. Even at his advanced age they expect a full recovery and the hemiparesis to subside. In the hospital he is inert. And yet troublesome. He wants to go home.

He yells at the girls in English, Take me to my wife. He says, Sarah will get lost. Sarah will get lonely.

Maude watches the old man bitching at a nurse trying to coax him into taking a sedative. The red-rimmed, watery eyes, the eyebrows feral and wild. His hands are still huge but clawed by arthritis and the skin is thinned and spotted. She remembers when she was little. She loved to squeeze between him and the couch cushions. Sit on me, Papa. He would lean back, and the crush made her feel safe. She would lie behind him, wrapped around him like a life preserver and they would watch TV like that. But she remembers that a single harsh word barked from him would bring her to tears. She'd be embarrassed by her tears, which would make her cry more. Her mom would comfort her and tell her that he didn't mean it. She was the same when her father yelled. Maude remembers vowing never to let a man raise his voice to her.

Zed tells him that his impromptu interment of their mother meant they had to fudge some paperwork. If anyone asks, they buried her at sea. He sees what he is doing to Zed. Her mother gave her milk. He fed her anxieties. So, she frets. From his bedroom, over the next few days, he listens to her fighting with unmoved administrators, notaries, attorneys. Occasionally she turns on Maude who, like a toreador, knows how to swivel and shift around her sister's moods.

The door to his bedroom opens. The light switch flips. The room brightens with ugly yellow light. No one enters. The girls are making breakfast. The man hears ABBA playing. It's pancakes. They are making offerings to Sarah, their mother. They want him to join them.

He groans loudly and dramatically.

The papa monster is awake, one of them says. He can't tell which. He took pills to sleep an empty dreamless sleep, but death will not be cheated of its grief, and the days after these sleeps are especially bleak. If it wasn't for this, he'd take the pills more often.

Monsieur Macgeeness, Maude says in a deep dramatic voice. She often addresses him by his last name, and he still finds it annoying. A demotion from Papa.

Are you getting up? Zed is making Mum's chestnut pancakes, she says in French. Maude, especially, always found French the easier language to exist in. For years, their English pronunciation still had the cockney twang of their birthplace, and he missed it when that leached away.

Maude sits in the man's wheelchair. She has pinned

up her two plaits in a laurel crown like Sarah used to do. They are so much her and not her that it unbalances him.

He struggles to sit up. The right arm is still weak, but he stubbornly does it himself. His daughter knows not to fuss. She watches the old man. She is good at holding the sadness at bay. How did he get so old? She resents that her memories will be tainted by this withered and furious creature. What will become of him now that her mum is dead? She doesn't think he'll last long. He'll give up and will himself to die. She should talk to Zed about arranging a nurse. Maude switches to English.

Hey, old man, I'm only here for a few more days. I'm going to miss you. And you are going to miss me. Snap out of it, yeah?

The man adjusts his pillow. He points to his water glass as he stifles a cough. She hands it to him and pops his morning pills from their blister pack for him. He takes a drink, holding the glass with both hands.

You want some coffee?

He sits, staring forward.

She reaches over and puts her forefinger on his chin. She feels the cat-tongue prickle of his beard.

She moves her finger up and down and ventriloquises the old man, mimicking the deep growl of his voice.

Good morning. Well, if it isn't my favourite daughter Maudie. Coffee? Pancakes, you say. I'm famished. Yes, thank you. Be right there. Could you possibly bring me some clothes so I can get dressed? Got to get up. I can't just sit here like a sad. Little. Toady man.

She takes his hand, still a little floppy, and puts it to her cheek.

You're running out of working limbs, she says.

He brushes his thumb against the softness. She kisses his hand before using it to smack his own face a few times.

Stop hitting yourself, Papa, she says. Why are you hitting yourself?

He laughs, calls her a penis. She gets up from his chair, kisses his head and goes to his dresser.

I love you and your sister. Equally, he says.

Sure, sure, old man, Maude says, delivering fresh clothes. Shout if you need any help.

Maude leaves with lots of tears and promises to return in a month. She is sad but relieved to leave the house, the life, the country of her childhood. On their first night without her, Zed and the old man play cribbage but after that they retreat into their own grieving. They both navigate by the watered-down light that manages to get through the windows. They sleep in late, go to bed early, from the exhaustion of moving through the thick dull air that hangs in the house.

On a day of full sun with a sky so blue it feels as though at least one problem in the world has been solved, Zed opens all the windows and doors to the house. In the breeze, Sarah's neglected house plants drop leaves that chase each other through the house like kittens. The man watches a manuscript left ignored on his bedside table. A page lifts and flutters until it has enough courage, goaded by the snap of the curtains, to jump to the floor. It glides freely across the tiles towards the open front door. Page by page, he watches the book he was working on leave him. He wheels across it to take a shower. Zed has cleaned the bathroom, and the towels have all been washed with some flouncy detergent that reminds him of the soap they use in resort hotels. He can't find his razor or shaving oil. When he comes out to grumble at her, she is at the kitchen sink pouring out a full bottle of vodka.

What the hell are you doing?

I can't have this in the house.

It's my booze, not yours. There are other people in the damn world besides you, he shouts. The anger is invigorating, a novelty amid the unrelenting emptiness he has felt since the morning his wife died. He continues, Stop messing with my house. You moved out to do fuck knows in London. Fuck knows except we still seem to be paying the bills for it.

Zed does not defend herself, but cries against his attack.

He wants to say that he knew her mom longer. Loved her first. He wants to hurt. To get this ache from his chest and put in the heart of his own daughter. She flees to her room and he, disgusted with himself, goes to his.

That night it is her who feels she should apologise. She makes one of his favourite dishes. Something her mum always made. The rattle of the pasta roller reminds Zed of all the times she cooked beside her mum. How many times she watched her father taking a bite, doing his happy wiggle and pouring out exaggerated expressions of praise for food they had made. He would go over to her mother's side of the table and kiss her. He would joke, Good news, girls! I've decided to keep your mom around for another year.

She knows her mum's tortellini en brodo recipe by heart and, like her mum, she eyes the measurements. The freezer holds jars of her mum's homemade stock. The handwriting on the label puts a lump in her throat. She hesitates, as if using them would delete her mum more than she already is. As she rolls out the pasta, she sees the old man in his spot next to the fairy fort. He has a book open, but Sais Pas has taken its place on top of it. His lips are moving as he pets the sleeping cat. He is talking to her mum. She is jealous of that.

She calls her father from the window, Dinner will be ready soon. She can't shake the fear that he is trying to die. That a part of him is selfishly revelling in his grief. She chastises herself for the cruelty of this thought, but she needs her father right now. She will tell him what she needs to tell him tonight.

She calls to him a few more times. This is usually the cue for whoever isn't cooking to set the table. Annoyed, she sets the table herself. Then goes to him and tells him dinner is ready. When he says he is not hungry, she finds herself yelling.

You need to stop right now. Stop trying to make me feel like shit. She was my mum for fuckssake. Do you remember what you were like after Momo died, huh? We practically carried you from room to room for a year. Get in the fucking house and eat the fucking dinner that I made you.

She marched back into the house shouting, Arsehole.

She is eating and does not look up when he pulls up to the table. He takes her wrist and throws apologies over the fire of her. He tries to please her and forces himself to eat, telling her how good it is. Sarah would be proud.

They are washing the dishes together when the richness of the meal hits him. The suddenness of it surprises them both. Zed jumps back as he is sick in the sink. He pulls a muscle, and she puts him to bed before returning to the kitchen to clean up his mess.

That night Sarah wakes him up by sitting on his bed.

Did I wake you?

It's okay. Your hair looks nice. I miss you.

I miss you.

She smiles. He scoots over and she lies down and puts her leg over him. He puts his hand on her thigh and gives it a squeeze.

I'm sorry for all the times I yelled at you.

There weren't many.

I wish there weren't any though. There wasn't enough time.

We had . . . What year were we married?

I don't remember either, the man says, smiling.

There is never enough time.

I'm worried about Zed.

Your daughter needs to tell you something.

I know. I'm trying but—

Listen. She is pregnant. She's keeping the baby and has decided to raise it alone, but she's scared. She's scared to tell you. She needs you to be Papa, to support her.

I want to stay here with you.

You can't.

My life has been can't.

Wah wah. I'm a wheelchair man that has two perfect daughters who love him. Wah wah.

You sound like Maudie.

The old man in the wheelchair is at his window tracing the blackened stripe along one of the cliffs to the south.

Someone started a forest fire in the calanques, he shouts to his daughter.

The cicadas are loud this morning, she replies distractedly. He feels her nervous energy behind him without looking back at her. She hasn't sat still all morning. The pines have been burned all the way down to the topaz of the Mediterranean. The colours are striking. Several threads of smoke rise across the horizon.

Joyriders were busy this weekend too, he comments.

Zed doesn't reply. She is cleaning an already clean kitchen. She makes herself a coffee, sits down to drink it. Back up again.

Hey, fussass, walk down to the beach with me? the old man asks. He tells her he was unable to sleep and watched a jellyfish bloom make each wave glow milky blue and that he wants to see all that gooey creepiness for himself.

As teenagers the girls used to dare each other to swim out to the collapsed Ferris wheel that marked where the beach used to be when they first moved to France.

Today the beach and a few hundred meters of the sea are blanketed by mauve jellyfish. It looks like an undulating laminate floor. It is grotesque and beautiful and happens a few times each year now.

You never used the callipers, she says pushing his wheelchair along the path.

I don't trust robots.

I think you just like people pushing you.

True also.

This is going to stink so much, she says.

Do you feel the red tide? he coughs.

They pick a spot along the sea wall. The man pats his daughter's leg and asks her, What's up? You've got something on your mind.

Her cheeks flush and she looks away. She wipes her face and takes a breath.

The man says, I appreciate you taking care of me. I'm sorry I'm such a shit sometimes. Thank you.

Do you remember when we moved? I had to change schools mid-year, and I was struggling. It was the same year that something with the planes kept making them crash. Do you remember?

I remember the planes.

She fixes a lose curl on her father's forehead.

I was getting bullied every day. I hated my teachers.

He shakes his head. The year of the planes?

You just cared about my grades. You told me only a moron fails high school. You wouldn't listen. I was so mad at you.

I had no idea. I'm sorry. Was this 2029?

I don't know. Yeah, maybe, probably. I already felt awful, and you made me feel worse.

Those years were . . . We had to move and change schools because . . . well, things were bad, and the planes falling out of the sky made it feel like the end of the world. I'm sorry I wasn't there for you, but I remember you doing really good at that school.

I did good to spite you. It wasn't just then. You never took my side or gave me a break. It was always 'suck it up', 'get tough'. You're so dismissive of everyone else's problems. You always threw it in my face how easy my life was.

It was easy.

See. Stop. Maybe. But it wasn't easy for me. Sometimes, I just needed you to agree that it was all bullshit. Take my side.

You did it though.

I was always going to do good, but I could have done it without feeling lousy the whole time. Maudie was the only person who knew how bad it was. She stopped me from hurting myself.

He hugs her and apologises.

I'm pregnant.

He tries to play surprised, You're kidding me. How far along? You've had your first scans, right? I'm so happy. Really?

Yes, I'm twelve weeks. So far everything looks good.

The statistical likelihood of a miscarriage drops off after twelve weeks, the old man recites.

That's not actually true any more. I haven't told anyone else. Except Maudie, she knows.

Have I met the dad?

He's not really a part of the plan.

He had some part, he says, but seeing her face drop, he stops. Sorry, what's your plan?

I wasn't sure. I was going to ask you and Mom if I could move back home but that was before—

Of course. Whatever you need, kiddo. I'm excited! Are you excited?

I think so.

I'm excited.

A woman stops to ask Zed if she is okay while the man with her looks away embarrassed.

Zed wipes her cheeks and with annoyance in her voice, says, Yes, I'm fine, thank you.

What was that about?

Hell if I know. I found videos of Mum on my old Kidi-Secrets diary. Do you want to watch them?

Somewhere in the universe, a particle died. A mote of existence became no more. Then another. Another, and the death of the universe began. The old man, unaware that the universe has ended, is in his bed waiting for his grandson to wish him good night. The little boy bounds onto the duvet, but he knows to be careful. His grandpa has told him he is old, delicate, made of stale crackers and the bubble gum from under park benches. His grandpa says lots of funny things and stories that are not true. The heat of the boy's small body is a comfort to the old man. The pain subsides as the boy settles into the nook of his arm and rubs at the scratch of the grey wires on his grandpa's chin.

His daughter's firstborn is a green-eyed, black-haired son. The old man in the wheelchair often feels guilty that he has the better part of the bargain. Having his daughter in the house helps salve a loneliness he is never quite prepared for. It swallows him sometimes and he knows it scares his daughters. The old man revels in the simplicity of his love for his grandson without all the frets and fears he knew as a parent. It's the easiest love of his life. The little boy never got to meet his grandma. When that thought returns, he can't help but react, and the little boy asks if he is okay.

Crazy pain, the man says.

The boy asks where it hurts then gives his grandpa's knee a kiss.

Six years on, to think about his wife, is to ache. The loss never lessened; they lied to him about that. Like the electric fire in his legs, his crazy pain, he is better at distracting himself from the cloying pull that her death brought. He is compelled, while he can, to tell the little boy where he comes from and hopes it gets him to where he needs to go. A vain wish, but when has vanity stopped a man?

Do you want to hear a story about your grandma?

Papi, will there be sadness?

Yes, that can't be helped, but joy too. That okay?

The boy nods.

Your grandmother was one of the last witches of the small magic. Maybe small magic isn't such a good name. Discreet magic, that better? Do you know what discreet means? What's that? Witches aren't scary. It used to be a word that meant wise woman, but for lots of years men feared women's power, so they made the word mean something bad. It is only the women of our family that make the small magic. The men you come from existed too much in this world to make the small magic. No, men aren't bad. Your grandpa is a man. Am I bad? That's nice of you, thank you. Yes, I love you too. Thank you. What's big magic? Wait now, I haven't even told you what the small magic is.

Zed comes and lies down on the other side of the old man. She pets her son and rests her hand on her father's, rough and hardened from pushing a wheelchair for most of his life. Still huge compared to hers. His nails need a trim, she thinks. And his hair, a wash.

He pats her hand. His health continues to decline, and she has too readily and too easily taken care of him despite having the little one as well. His most recent surgery has brought only new pain, new weakness. She insists that being here, helping him, is what she wants to do, but he feels guilty, nonetheless. He finds the hospice nurse annoyingly chipper but submits to his ministrations for Zed's sake. Because of the old man's accent, age and disability, the nurse has assumed that he is a veteran. The old man entertains himself by making up war stories from half-remembered episodes of the TV show *M*A*S*H*.

Kid knows what discreet means, the father says to his daughter.

Of course, his mom's a genius.

Your mom doesn't think we should talk about the small magic, but I'm old so I don't have to follow rules any more. Your great-grandma and your great-great-grandma and your great-great-great-grandma were witches of the small magic too. There's a lot of magic in our family. You're a very lucky boy. Some day, when you need it, you'll have the small magic to protect you.

I'm crying a little, yes. I miss your grandma and talking about her sometimes reminds me of that. Well, it's better than not crying about someone. Yes, your mom and aunt Maudie have the small magic.

The boy pokes at the tear on his grandpa's cheek.

That true? the boy asks his mother. She smiles and nods. The boy looks between the adults measuring the exchange, knowing he is not understanding everything.

Okay, well, let me think. Your aunt Maudie was littler than you are now. Maybe four. It started with terrible nightmares. She said ghosts were coming and wanted her to follow them. They wanted to take her away. This went on for a few more nights. Then she started sleepwalking. That was scary. One night she was trying to open the front door, but she was too small for the top lock. When we found her, she said she was going with them. Her eyes were wide open, but she was still asleep.

The old man ignored his daughter's silent pleading not to tell scary stories before bed.

After your grandma put her back to bed, she got an oil and dabbed it on your aunt Maudie's forehead like this.

He touches the boy's temples.

No, I don't know what was in it. Ask your mom. See, she won't tell us boys. Probably for the best. Then your grandma took an empty jar. She put the top on then wrapped it with twine. She used the twine to fix a little twig to the jar. She put this contraption underneath Maudie's bed and each night her nightmares were less and less. At the end of the week, I saw your grandma pull the jar out from under Maudie's bed. It was still sealed up with twine but that little twig had sprouted leaf buds, and the jar was full of black, sticky, wet soil. She took the twig and twine and wrapped it against the trunk of the tree outside what's now your bedroom, and poured out the dirt against its trunk. You can see it for yourself tomorrow morning. There's one branch, real low, that has different leaves than the rest of the tree. No, it's late, we'll have a look tomorrow. What's that? Yes, when your grandma died, I was right beside her. The old man sees his daughter trying to warn him not to fall into a maudlin tale about her mother as he is apt to do. We were at the mountain house. Yes, we should go up there soon. When it gets a little hotter, we will. Your grandma and me were sitting out in the back garden. Your grandma turned to me and said that she was sorry, but it was time for her to go. She said that she was sad that it had to be on such a beautiful day. She had no more magic left. She thanked me for the good life we had together. She told me about you before your mom did. She knew. That's the small magic for you. She knew you'd be a clever, handsome boy who would make us all proud.

What a family of criers we are, Zed says, sniffing.

They both chuckle, before the man continues, Grandma made me promise to not be so sad that I couldn't be a good grandpa for you. What do you think? Did I do a good job at being Grandpa? Thanks. When I see Grandma next, I'll let her know you said so. Good night.

Soon after, the old man in the wheelchair dies. Late one night he and his daughters are sitting at the long wooden table that Sarah had dreamed of for years. It is stained and scratched with memories. Underneath, it is covered in messages and the names of everyone who visited the house. He talks about the days when Zed and Maude were young and the house was packed full of feral teenagers, always too loud. How annoying it was at the time, how much he misses it, and how it will be that way again in ten years when her son brings his friends around. The old man asks his daughters to leave the 'hospice care kit' in the fridge beside his bed tonight. He wants to go on his own terms. While he still has the strength. Zed understands but can't bring herself to say yes.

Remember when we lived in London and, when we took walks, we played 'muck or turd' with the stuff on the pavement.

The old man smiles.

This one is a turd.

They all chuckle.

They spend the night trading stories of each other. Like the time Maude at thirteen only spoke to the old man in French but with a thick German accent. It drove him up the wall at the time. Or when the girls figured out what the wet wipes on their parents' bedside were for.

Ick, don't even mention that, Zed laughs.

Maude says, If someone said a person was ugly, you'd always say, You don't make babies with your face.

Momo used to say that, he says.

What's that even mean?

When they say good night, the old man kisses and hugs his daughters for the last time. He tells each one that she was always his favourite. After he goes to bed, Maude says he had it as good as it gets. To die a few years after your life partner, at a time of your choosing. For a grumpy cripple that man had a charmed life.

The sisters will not be able to sleep and will sit at the table, knowing what is happening in the bedroom down the hall. After the old man's death, each woman will dream of their father.

Acknowledgements

First and foremost, thank you Debbie Bogard.

I'd like to thank Arts Council England, who funded the live literature project *In Billions of Years, the Sun Will Swallow the Earth*, which became the heart of this book and to *Hinterland* magazine, who published the text version in their issue #12. Thanks to Andy Sewell and Ed Prosser, my collaborators on the project, and the rector of St Matthews Church of Bethnal Green, Erin Clark, for hosting us.

To the Eccles Centre & Hay Festival Writer's Award for the support, financial and creative. Especially to Polly Russell who always had time for one more question and always knew who might have the answer.

For your friendship and your knowledge in obstetrics, Anna McDougall.

To those patient and beautiful readers who saw versions of this book while I was still trying to understand it myself. Thank you to Christina Petrie, Kate Ellis, Ruth Harrison, Kira McPherson, Seth Oldmixon, Ben Platts-Mills, Riley Rockford, Nicolás Rodríguez Galvis, Sarah Sanders and the Willesden Green Writers' Group.

Lastly, thank you to my extended family, living and passed, for always being there and always telling stories.

Credits

Jarred McGinnis and Vintage would like to thank everyone who worked on the publication of *There Is No Meant To Be*

Agent

Will Francis

Editors

Kate Harvey

Ellie Steel

Editorial

Chris Sturtivant

Copy-editor

Luke Brown

Proofreader

Jane Howard

Managing Editorial

Graeme Hall

Contracts

Gemma Avery

Ceri Cooper

Rebecca Smith

Humayra Ahmed

Kiran Halaith

Anne Porter

Hayley Morgan

Harry Sargent

Design

Matt Broughton

Digital

Anna Baggaley

Claire Dolan

Brydie Scott

Charlotte Ridsdale

Zaheerah Khalik

Inventory

Rebecca Evans

Publicity

Aidan O'Neill

Finance

Ed Grande
Aya Daghem
Joseph Thomas

Production

Konrad Kirkham
Polly Dorner

Sales

Nathaniel Breakwell
Malissa Mistry
Justin Ward-Turner
Sarah Griffin
Ben Tapson
Lewis Cain
Nick Cordingly

Kate Gunn
Sophie Dwyer
Maiya Grant
Danielle Appleton
Phoebe Edwards
Amber Blundell
Rachel Cram
David Atkinson
Amanda Dean
Andy Taylor
Dan Higgins

Rights

Lucy Beresford-Knox
Celia Long
Beth Wood
Annamika Singh
Agnes Watters
Lucie Deacon
Liv Diomedes
Jake Dickson

Audio

Nile Faure-Bryan